TRUMP:
THE PRISON DIARIES

Also by Lucien Young

Alice in Brexitland

Trump's Christmas Carol

The Secret Diary of Jeremy Corbyn

#Sonnets

The Secret Diary of Boris Johnson Aged 13¼

The Downing Street Guide to Party Etiquette

Elon Musk (Almost) Saves the World

TRUMP:

THE PRISON DIARIES

An unpresidented tale of endurance, redemption and fake tan.

Written by Donald J. Trump,
45th President of the United States,
who is great at words – the best, in fact.
Many people are saying this, believe me.

Edited by the failing Lucien Young
– very unfair to Trump

WILDFIRE

First published in 2023 by
WILDFIRE
an imprint of HEADLINE PUBLISHING GROUP

2

Line illustrations courtesy of iStock/Getty Images
(© abbydesign, nosyrevy, FrankRamspott, carlacdesign,
Natasha_Pankina, Nikiteev_Konstantin)

Cataloguing in Publication Data is available from the British Library

Hardback ISBN 978 1 0354 1121 4

Designed and set by EM&EN
Printed and bound in Great Britain by Clays Ltd, Elcograf S.p.A.

Headline's policy is to use papers that are natural, renewable and recyclable
products and made from wood grown in well-managed forests and other
controlled sources. The logging and manufacturing processes are expected
to conform to the environmental regulations of the country of origin.

HEADLINE PUBLISHING GROUP
An Hachette UK Company
Carmelite House
50 Victoria Embankment
London EC4Y 0DZ

www.headline.co.uk
www.hachette.co.uk

Men are not prisoners of fate, but only
prisoners of their own minds.

>   – Franklin Delano Roosevelt

Every true hustler knows that you
cannot hustle forever. You will go to jail
eventually.

>   – The Notorious B.I.G.

Foreword

Everyone remembers where they were when they heard the news. Donald Trump, formerly the world's most powerful man, had been found guilty. The tangerine tyrant was headed for the slammer. He would be swapping the White House for the big house, Mar-a-Lago for the hoosegow. Not since Richard Nixon had anyone dreamed of a president in pokey. It was mind-blowing. Surreal. And very much in keeping with events since 2016.

Reactions were predictable, given Trump's polarising nature. Democrats applauded the strength of the US legal system. Republicans decried this conspiracy by globalist elites. Blue states rejoiced, sounding the horns of their Priuses and sipping mimosas at brunch. Red states howled, sounding the horns of their pick-up trucks and firing AR-15s in the air. Late-night comedians crowed and wept and occasionally made jokes. The influencers of the MAGAsphere ranted and raged and shared links to crowdfunding pages. There was talk of a violent insurrection but none materialised. Then everybody got distracted when it came out that Taylor Swift was dating Pete Davidson. This was all to be expected.

What no one expected was that, during his confinement, President Trump would keep a diary. Nevertheless, he did just that, penning thousands of words on several rolls of toilet paper. The Donald has been called many things, but literary is not one of them. Perhaps his separation from social media forced him to go long-form. In any case, the resulting entries offer unparalleled access to Trump's mind. Not only do they grant us fascinating insight into the psychological effects of his captivity, they demonstrate the day-to-day life of a modern American prison.

How do I know all this? Because, mere weeks ago, a package containing the chronicle landed on my doorstep. Accompanying the reams of toilet tissue (unused, for which I am grateful) was a note in Trump's hand. It demanded, in his inimitable style, that I, Lucien Young, edit the enclosed diaries and prepare them for publication. Why he would give this job to an author of humour books, I do not know. But I did my best to oblige, using the latest technology to decipher his childlike scrawl. While I may not agree with Trump on many – or indeed any – issues, I felt compelled to preserve this text for future historians. There was also money involved.

Of course, the reader is aware of the shocking conclusion to Trump's prison odyssey. One would have to live under a rock not to be. A rock without WiFi. Still, the following chapters contain their share of twists and turns, thrills and spills, harrowing revelations and wild reversals of fortune. And at the centre of it all is the orange enigma that commands the world's attention to this day. A human megaphone whose grasping digits and gravity-defying coiffure are known from Afghanistan to Zimbabwe. A guy who, more than anyone, has reshaped politics in his own twisted image.

You may think Trump was crazy before his incarceration. Friend, you ain't seen nothing yet.

Lucien Young

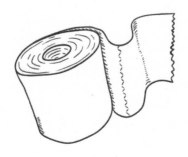

Contents

Part Three: The Smallhand Redemption

PART ONE

PRISONER #42069

What separates the winners from the losers is how a person reacts to each new twist of fate.

> – Donald Trump,
> *Surviving at the Top*, 1990

1

Orange is the New Orange

HORRIBLE! UNFAIR! SAD!

This is, frankly, the greatest injustice in the history of America. It's bad, folks, very bad. In fact, it's worse than bad. It's not good.

I, Donald J. Trump, 45th President of the United States and highly successful billionaire, have been locked up. They locked me up even though I did nothing wrong. Ever. No crimes, no collusion, *nada*. But try telling that to the communist Democrats and lying fake-news media, who are both so awful for our country.

I'd say the charges were trumped up, but I don't like that term. It's more like they were Obama-ed up. Or Bidened up. The trial was rigged, just like the 2020 election. I was told I would be tried by a jury of my peers. But how could they be my peers? Not a single one of them was a billionaire. Or even a millionaire. You could tell from their outfits. Men in polo shirts, women wearing sweaters – no glamour! Why don't people have style these days, like they did in the eighties?

It's clear the judge – a very biased psycho – was a fan of Crooked Hillary Clinton. Like all liberals, she was unattractive, a four or five at best. And, boy, did she hate Trump. You could tell she was getting off every time she banged that gavel (which looked very cheap, by the way – not classy, like a Trump-brand gavel would be[*]).

I had to sit in the courtroom, listening to low-energy attorneys make their arguments. Actually, I didn't listen. I just sat there, scowling, so people would think I was paying attention. But really I was daydreaming about me and Bo Derek on a desert island. Very erotic. Tremendous. I still caught a few things the prosecutor said, though. 'Willful malfeasance'. 'Egregious corruption'. 'Contempt for the law, democracy and basic decency'. BORING!

After weeks of this crap, they reached a verdict. I hate long sentences, whether in court or written down. The one they gave me was a doozy, a real beaut. On the bright side, my trial was televised and got amazing ratings. Trump is BOX OFFICE DYNAMITE! It truly is incredible that NBC ditched me as host of *The Apprentice*. How stupid are they?

---

[*] Note to self: look into selling Trump gavels. And Trump gravel. And maybe Trump anvils.

Now I'm sitting here in a cell. Not even a luxury, executive cell, with twenty-four-carat bars and a king-sized cot. Just a normal cell for losers. It's about six feet by eight feet, nowhere near big enough for an athletic guy like me. The mattress is hard, lumpy, in no way deluxe. There's a toilet-sink dealie sticking out of the wall – stainless steel, not solid gold like my toilets at home. I have the best bathrooms there. Marble floors. Golden showers. Top-of-the-line hand wash. Plus, they're spacious enough to hold thousands of classified documents.

The level of service here is unbelievable. And I mean bad unbelievable, not good unbelievable. The guards treat me like some kind of criminal. They won't even let me watch TV. How am I meant to get through the day without six hours of Fox News? I need red-faced guys and hot blondes plastered in makeup. They keep me informed about how brilliant I am, how badly I've been treated and how everyone who doesn't like Trump is a flag-burning sicko.

I need Sean Hannity on my screen, yelling about how Mexicans want to take our guns and change our pronouns or whatever. Without that, I start thinking my own thoughts. And thinking thoughts is a bad deal for me. Because then I might regret stuff, or remember my childhood, or hear my dad's voice telling me I'll never be enough. I say drown it all out. Self-reflection? No thank you.

So to occupy my brain – which is a first-class brain, not at all fucked up – I have decided to keep a diary. It will be a beautiful diary. Terrific. Very entertaining. When it gets published, it will sell more copies than the Bible, or even *The Art of the Deal*. People will say Trump is the greatest diarist of all time, way better than that wig-wearing loser Samuel Pepys. Or Anne Frank, who, to be fair, was treated pretty rough. That was a rough deal. Nearly as bad as what's happening with me.

Most importantly, it will give a full and honest account of my time behind bars. The American people – and even people too dumb to be born American – will bear witness to this terrible perversion of justice. And when I get out – any day now, believe me, all the experts are saying – they will see that Trump was tough. Tougher, in fact, than Charles Bronson and Jean-Claude Van Damme put together.

Therefore I, Donald J. Trump, hereby commence my diary, which I duly execute, with great presidentialism, effective immediately.

DAY ONE

I sat in the gray prison bus, wearing a steel collar and chains. These rattled every time we went over a pothole, which was about once a second. Outside, Florida swampland sped past. Brown, bleak, depressing. To think this was the same state where I lived, in the magnificent Mar-a-Lago. Where I built the Trump International Golf Course, West Palm Beach, rated one of the top golf courses in Florida by the prestigious *Florida Golf Magazine*. Where rich guys go to enjoy themselves – the best people, like me and Jeffrey Epstein.

It was the first time in years I had been in a vehicle that wasn't a chopper, a private jet or a limo. All around me sat hardened crooks. We're talking the lowest of the low: drug dealers, murderers, men with tattoos. I never trust anybody with a tattoo. Unless it's Dennis Rodman, who was so good on *Celebrity Apprentice*. The point is, these guys were bad news. They were parasites who took from society without giving anything back. They had no compassion or regard for their fellow man. And they were happy to break the law if it fulfilled their own selfish needs. What was I, Donald Trump, doing among them?

'There she is,' said the guy next to me.

I looked out the barred window to see

our destination: Smallhand State Prison. As someone in the construction business, I can tell you it's a horrible building. A big stone tumor on the landscape. Whoever the developer was had zero class. Come to think of it, the government should let me build Trump Prisons. These would be swanky, chic, very exclusive, with slot machines, Jacuzzis and chandeliers in every cell. You could have different membership tiers, from Gold Con to Double-platinum Diamond-encrusted Super-premium Con.

But maybe that wouldn't be such a good idea. Everybody would be committing crimes just so they could get in. They would rip the country apart to gain access to the luxury with which Trump is synonymous.

Anyway, the bus rumbled into the prison and the gates closed behind us. I was surrounded on all sides by tall, dark walls. Now, I famously love walls. But these ones? Not so much. Because they weren't there to keep Mexicans out. They were there to keep me in. Suddenly I felt extra not great.

We were led off the bus, chained together single file. Inmates ran up to a chain-link fence, shaking it and yelling at us: 'Fresh fish! Fresh fish! Hey, fishy, fishy, fishy! We're gonna have a lot of fun with you, little fishies!'

I just stuck out my jaw and scowled extra hard. I wasn't scared. I came up in New York real estate, dealing with tough, vicious guys. I mean killers. Not actual killers, like some of these guys are. But still.

Somebody shouted, 'A-yo, is that Trump? Goddamn, it is him! Look at his skin – shit's like Day-Glo Orange!'

I winced as the cons at the fence started jeering, saluting and singing 'Hail to the Chief'. Usually I love attention, but I didn't love this kind. A man with a skull tattooed over his face smiled at me, revealing gold teeth.

'Welcome to Smallhand, Mr President!'

Guards marched us into a huge, drab room and took off our collars and chains. One of them stepped forward, slapping his baton against the palm of his hand.

'Okay, maggots!' he screamed. 'Take off all your clothes!'

I wasn't happy. Not because I'm in any way ashamed of my body. I'm actually a perfect physical specimen. A lot of bodybuilders tell me, 'Sir, those are the finest pecs I've ever seen.' So I wasn't self-conscious. I just didn't want to undress in front of these felons. The sight of me naked is a gift I have given to only a few hundred beautiful women. And my doctors, of course. Who all agree that I am in incredible shape and that it's big, medically speaking.

I was shoved into a steel cage and blasted with a fire hose. The water was freezing and the pressure so high it made my body – which is very muscular – jiggle like a bowl of Jell-O. After this came another kick in the teeth. A guard threw a pile of white powder over me, making my eyes burn. I spent a lot of time at Studio 54 in the seventies, so I'm used to piles of white powder.* But this wasn't cocaine – I was being deloused. Look, Trump would never have lice. And if I did, they would be the best lice, the classiest lice, believe me.

That wasn't the worst thing. The worst thing was when they made me bend over and had a good, long look up my ass. Checking for contraband, they said. Money, drugs, stuff like that. I think they were just perverts. And I'm a hundred percent straight, okay? It's outrageous to suggest I would put anything up there. I won't even see a proctologist.

Finally, I was given a number – 42069 – and they put me in a bright orange jumpsuit. As I was led to my cell, I caught my reflection in a window. For the first time in my life, I didn't look tremendous. The jumpsuit was the exact same shade as my face (Neon Pumpkin, according to color charts). You couldn't tell where it ended and I began. How had this happened to the world's leading style icon? For years, fashionable men from New York

---

* I never took any, though. The only Coke I'm into is Diet.

to Milan had copied my giant, boxy suits and extremely long ties. Now I looked like a slob. It was as though they were trying to take away my identity.

The guards deposited me in a crummy little cell and slammed the bars behind me. I didn't have a TV, a phone or even a magazine, so I spent the next few hours making a mental list of everyone who has ever wronged me. James Comey. Rosie O'Donnell. The cast and crew of *Saturday Night Live*. It truly is strange I have so many enemies when I'm such a nice guy. Eventually, a guard shouted, 'Sweet dreams, ladies!' The lights clanked off, one after another, leaving us all in darkness.

They say your first night in jail is the hardest and, sure, it was no picnic. A less macho guy might have cried. But I didn't, not once. I haven't cried since I was a baby. If you shed a tear, even when you're alone, your credibility is shot. Your enemies will sense weakness and they will attack. Crying is for losers and homos. Plus, it makes your tan run.

So, yeah, my eyes remained one hundred percent dry. There was no sobbing whatsoever. If any of the guys in my cell block say otherwise, they're lying. Also, I have reason to believe they're in the pocket of George Soros and the Clinton Crime Family. Sad!

Anyway, I woke up around 5 a.m., like I usually do. During my White House days, I would sit on the toilet for about an hour and fire off tweets. On this occasion, I grabbed some toilet paper and the pen I'd smuggled in beneath one of my chins. One of my very manly chins. I then used the morning light to write the above entries. Today is my first full day on the inside. Hopefully my guards and fellow inmates will start treating me with the respect I deserve.

DAY TWO

I wasn't crazy about being in prison. Now I'm officially pissed off.

Before I even had a chance to settle in, they put me to work. And not in a job worthy of my talents, like CEO, President of the United States or participant in WWE's WrestleMania. No, they stuck me in the prison laundry. I had to spend hours working my ass – which is very neat and muscular – off, cleaning prisoners' underwear stained with God knows what. The industrial washers and presses made the room hot as hell, causing me to sweat like Li'l Marco Rubio. The noise was deafening and I couldn't hear myself think. To be honest, I didn't mind that last part.

Next it was time for the showers. I stood in a bare concrete room with, like, a dozen guys as little shower heads dribbled on us. The cold made my prick shrink down to a nub. I considered stroking it and thinking of Brigitte Bardot, so as not to look bad in front of the other prisoners. Then I realized they might misunderstand the gesture. A friend told me you should never drop the soap in prison showers. I told him that wasn't a problem, because I'm physically incapable of bending over.

At Smallhand, the highlight of the day – if you can call it that – is exercise period. Cons wander around the yard, occasionally throwing a baseball back and forth. I was captain of the baseball team in high school. Some said I was the best player in New York state. Probably because my hands are so big, which made catching a piece of cake. But I refuse to play now. I don't want these hoodlums thinking we're on the same level.

They say that on your first day in prison, you should find the biggest guy and hit him in the face. I considered this, but decided against it. I'm incredibly strong and, even if I pull my punch, there's a good chance I'd kill the guy. Then I'd never get out. So I will only use my physical might in exceptional circumstances. You've got to be strong, but you've got to be smart.

As horrible as my first day was, the meals were the low point. Honestly, the mess hall is a MESS. It's worse than one of sissy Graydon Carter's bad food restaurants. You line up to get a scoop of glop, then sit at a cafeteria table, listening to thugs chew at unbelievable volume. The crap they serve is disgusting. Anyone would find it hard to choke down, but I'm used to the very finest cuisine. Trump steaks, well done and smothered in ketchup. McDonald's Filet-O-Fish with many, many French fries. And, of course, delicious hamberders. You won't find that stuff here. They even make you eat vegetables.

The drink situation isn't any better. They expect us to drink water. What am I, a horse? I haven't drunk water in fifty years. When I was in the Oval Office, I had a special red button on my desk. I would press it – *boop* – and a White House butler would bring me a Diet Coke on a silver platter. I would drink twelve Diet Cokes a day, keeping me in great shape and giving me the energy I needed to make presidential decisions. Only problem is, my Coke button was right next to the nuclear button. That led to some hilarious mix-ups, I can tell you.

At lights out, I collapsed on my cot, alone with my thoughts. And some of those thoughts made me feel not so hot. I started asking myself tough questions. Did I bring this situation on myself? Could I have avoided it if I'd done things differently? Am I a fundamentally bad person, driven exclusively by greed? Has my only effect on the world been to make it a dumber, gaudier, less kind place?

No. No, that's crazy talk. I did nothing wrong. Everyone is just out to get me.

2

This Means Warden

DAY THREE

I was working on yesterday's entry when I heard footsteps approaching. I stuck the toilet paper under my mattress and hid the pen in my thick, golden mane. A guard – ugly, out of shape – appeared at the bars to find me looking very casual.

'Trump,' he said. 'Warden's office, now.'

I was led to a drab and boring office, nowhere near as nice as my office in Trump Tower. For instance, this one didn't have a magnificent view of Central Park, or contain Mike Tyson's championship belt and a shoe given to me by Shaquille O'Neal. The warden stood at a window overlooking the yard, staring out, hands clasped behind his back.

'Prisoner #42069,' he said, turning around. 'Thank you for joining me.'

'It didn't seem like I had a choice.'

He smiled, humorless.

'I am Jeremiah Snook, the warden here at Smallhand.'

With his beady eyes and short-cropped silver

hair, the guy reminded me of Mike Pence. Like Mike, he was a wacko Bible-thumper. I could tell from the crucifix on his wall, which was almost life-size. Hanging nearby was a framed quotation:

> It is easier for a camel to go through a needle's eye, than for a rich man to enter into the kingdom of God.
> – Luke 18:25

I let out a snort.

'Which pinko said that?'

Snook followed my gaze, then smiled tightly.

'That would be Jesus Christ, our Lord and Savior.'

Uh-oh, I thought. If I know one thing about Christians, it's that they get protective about this Jesus guy. He's almost like a messiah to them. I tried some damage control.

'Listen, I love the Jesus. What he's doing and what he's been doing, it's beautiful, truly. And I empathize. When he got up on that cross, it was like me getting made fun of at the White House Correspondents' Dinner. Or when Megyn Kelly asked me horrible, unfair questions at the Republican debate. In a way, I have it harder than Christ. He only had one Judas – I have

hundreds. One thing I'll say, though? Do we
really need a father, a son AND a Holy Ghost?
If I was in charge, I'd get it down to two. Same
level of service, much better value.'

Snook seemed satisfied with this.

'You make some interesting theological
points,' he said.

I felt relieved. The guy liked me. Of course
he did. He's an older white male with strong
religious views. In other words, a natural
MAGA type. It was all becoming clear – he'd
called me in to say I'm his hero and he would
make sure I had an easy time in his jail.

'No doubt you are wondering why I arranged
this meeting,' he said. 'Firstly, I want you to
know that you will receive no special privileges
in Smallhand. Your wealth and political
influence count for nothing here. You will work,
sweat and suffer like any other prisoner.'

What the hell, I thought. And also, What the
fuck?

'Secondly, I want you to know that I will be
watching you like a hawk. There is – I suppose
inevitably – considerable media interest in your
stay here. I will not allow you to embarrass
this institution or its staff. Put simply, your ass
belongs to me.'

He smiled again, this time sadistic. It didn't
make sense – I thought the guy was a God-
botherer.

'Why are you being so nasty?' I said.
'Evangelicals love Trump.'

'Not this evangelical. As far as I'm
concerned, you are nothing more than a sinner.
You are a fornicator and an adulterer—'

'That's right. With many beautiful women.'

'– in fact, you commit the seven deadly sins
on a daily basis.'

'Wrong! I'll cop to six of them – lust, greed,
pride, sleepy, bashful and doc. But not envy.
Trump doesn't envy anyone.'

Snook just glared at me.

'Think on your sins, Prisoner #42069. I'll be
seeing you.'

He nodded at the guards and I was led away.
This is why you can't trust religious guys. They
spend their time worshipping Jesus when they
should be worshipping Trump.

DAY FIVE

The number-one problem with jail is it's full
of crooks. I spend morning, noon and night
surrounded by jailbirds. These guys are
losers, no class. And don't get me wrong, I
have nothing against criminals. Some of my
best friends are criminals. But how stupid
do you have to be to get caught? Everyone
here claims they're the innocent victim of a

corrupt criminal-justice system. Firstly, that's ridiculous. Secondly, it's offensive, because I actually am the innocent victim of a corrupt criminal-justice system.

Not only are these cons losers, they're dangerous. Violence is always in the air. And I'm famous, maybe the most famous guy in the world, which puts a target on my back. Wherever I go, these animals call out to me:

'Mr Oompa Loompa!'

'Marmalade Man!'

'Orange Bitch!'

You can tell they would love to rough up the former president. Then they'd be the big guy in prison.

Trump doesn't get scared, but if I did, I'd be pissing my pants every time I saw a shadow. Especially because I wasn't allowed to bring my secret-service detail. So I'm thinking I need to get ripped. Swole, some people say. Not just for protection, but for my own state of mind. I want to feel like I'm achieving something in here. Imagine the faces of the haters and losers if Trump came out of jail with even more muscles than before. Like Schwarzenegger in his day, but twice as big.

Smallhand doesn't have a gym, so I decided to work out in my cell. A hundred sit-ups seemed like a good start. I lay down, put my hands behind my head and started to pull myself up. I realized I was in trouble immediately. Pain shot through me and my whole body started to spasm. I fell back, coughing, wheezing, drenched in sweat. Then I realized I couldn't get up. I had to lie there, like a huge orange turtle that had been flipped over, until a guard came and helped me two hours later.

It didn't make any sense. Back in 2015, my doctor – Harold Bornstein, the best in the business – released a letter saying, 'If elected, Mr Trump, I can state unequivocally, would be the healthiest individual ever elected to the presidency.' What had happened since then? I keep in great shape, frequently golfing (though I mainly stay in the cart) and drinking a gallon of Diet Coke a day. They wouldn't call it 'Diet' if it wasn't good for you.

The only explanation I can think of is that my enemies secretly injected me with some kind of weakening serum. Lots of people are saying this, and we're going to be looking into it very strongly. And, actually, half a sit-up is very impressive. A lot of Olympic athletes couldn't manage that.

DAY SEVEN

A guard came up to me as I kicked pebbles around the yard. He was a chinless mouth-breather who looked like a thumb and had a dumb southern accent. Unlike the other guards, he seemed kind of shy.

'Howdy, Mr Trump. I've been meaning to say hi, but it's taken me a while to get up the courage. See, I'm a big fan of yours. Huge.'

I glanced at his massive waist.

'I can see that.'

He laughed and ran a giant ham-hand across his buzzcut.

'Yeah, I could stand to lose a few pounds. The name's Clint. Clint Blorch. I'm the captain of the guards.'

I wanted to end this interaction as soon as possible. It's a funny thing, but as great as I am, my fans and supporters tend to be major slobs. I'm happy when they cheer for me at rallies from a safe distance, and agree to fund my many important ventures. But spending time with them? That's a no-no.

'Well, Clint, I've got a lot of rocks to kick, so—'

He started to get cute with me.

'Hey, I just had a crazy idea! I've got a ton of Trump merchandise at home. Maybe if I bring some in, you could sign it? Y'know, for me to give to friends and family. And also sell on eBay.'

This crossed a line. No one makes money off Trump except Trump.

'Yeah, I don't think I'll be doing—'

Clint's head snapped away from me. He started marching toward a group of cons crouched by the wall.

'Hey! Are you scumbags shooting dice? You know damn well there's no gambling in this place.'

One of them stood up. It was a guy I'd noticed in the mess hall, a skinny guy with a spider tattoo on his hand.

'Man, we're just playing,' he said. 'We ain't betting on—'

In a flash, Clint whipped out his baton and brought it down on the skinny guy's head. Skinny hit the ground like a sack of potatoes. The guard rained blows on him, red-faced and screaming.

'No gambling and no talking back! How'd you like that, you needle-dick, shit-sucking maggot?'

He stopped and turned to me, suddenly all smiles.

'So yeah, how about those autographs?'

I looked at him, then the guy twitching on the concrete. I gulped.

'That would be my pleasure.'

I've now been in here a whole week and I haven't had a single visitor. Why are my friends and family treating me like this? Could it be something I did? No, I've only ever been

kind, generous and loyal. There must be some
conspiracy to keep them away. I should have
paid more attention to that Q guy.

DAY EIGHT

I finally got a visitor. When the guards told me,
I ran to the visiting room as fast as I can (about
two miles an hour). There I found a series of
glass partitions with stools in front of them.
To the side of each partition hung a phone so
you could talk through it.

'Number six,' said a guard, pointing with his
baton.

When I saw the grinning face behind the
glass, my heart sank. It was my worst kid,
Don Jr.

Look, Trump has incredible genes. German
stock. But it's been hit-and-miss in terms of
children. There's my favorite, the gorgeous
Ivanka. There's Eric, a big-toothed simpleton
with milk-colored skin. There's Tiffany, who
everybody forgets about, myself included. And
then there's Barron, who I haven't talked
to much, but is nine feet tall, automatically
making him my second favorite. Some people
say you shouldn't rank your kids. Clearly their
parents didn't rank them highly.

Anyway, Don Jr is a total dud. Five kids, and the one I give my name to turns out worst. Go figure. His mother Ivana was a gorgeous Czech model. Beautiful. And of course I'm up there with Paul Newman and Robert Redford in terms of male attractiveness. So how did he turn out so weird-looking? He's got shiny skin, greasy hair and a little beard to cover up his lack of a chin. Then there's the way he talks – frantic, eager, like a puppy on cocaine. Sad!

With a shudder, I picked up the phone.

'Hey, Pops!' said Don Jr. 'It's fabulous to see you. I'd have come sooner, but I'm pretty busy running the Trump Organization and owning the libs on Twitter.'

I told him that if he's busy, he shouldn't worry about coming to see me, but he didn't get the hint. Not the brightest bulb.

'You look fantastic,' he said. 'Did you lose weight? Not that you needed to. I wish I had your body.'

It's embarrassing, frankly, how much my oldest son wants my approval. He even tries to act like me, squinting and waving his hands around. All I want is for him to be his own man. While also being totally obedient and asking my permission at every turn.

'How're you holding up?' he was saying. 'Real good, I bet. My dad is the toughest. Tougher than anyone else's dad.'

I replied with a small grunt. After a beat, he continued.

'I want you to know, I'm thinking about you every second of every day. I won't rest until I get you out of this hellhole.'

'Oh yeah?' I said. 'How are you going to do that?'

His dumb grin cut out for a second, then came back with a vengeance.

'Well, right now me and the boys on 4chan are cooking up some dank memes. Really epic stuff. There's this cartoon frog called Pepe and he—'

'Junior, what the hell are you talking about? How is a frog meant to spring me from jail?'

There was now panic in his eyes.

'Y'know, by raising awareness. Firing up the alt-right. They could post, send emails, maybe start a petition . . .'

He trailed off, looking miserable and even damper than usual. I just stared at him.

'Yeah, no, you're right – that plan is suboptimal. I should liaise with my people, restrategize our tactics. But I'm definitely across this, and the problem is close to being fixed. I promise I'll make you proud. I . . . I really love you, Pops.'

'Okay, that's time,' I said, hanging up the phone and walking away from the partition.

Anyway, I'm hoping I get some better visitors soon. Maybe my daughter, Ivanka, or my wife, Melania. God, that is one hot piece of ass. And Melania's not bad either.

3

Pleased to Eat You

DAY TEN

I woke up this morning shivering and sweating. There's no question I'm going through withdrawal symptoms. I feel anxious, nauseous, paranoid. My body itches all over. I would do anything, literally anything, for a fix. It has now been a week and a half since I used social media. I keep thinking of very smart things to say and reaching for my cellphone. But I don't have a cellphone in here. I don't even have pockets on my jumpsuit.

It used to be so good when I was on Twitter. The instant I had a thought about North Korea or Robert Pattinson's love life, I could blast it out to millions of people. No matter what I said, my replies would be full of messages of love and support from followers called @QAnonGrandma and @TheDiabeticPatriot. Then I got banned (unfairly) after January 6 – which was not my fault – and I moved to my own platform, Truth Social. The only people on there are MAGA whack jobs, meaning you don't get to fight with famous libs. Still, it was better than this.

By the way, I could go back on Twitter any time I want. When Creepy Elon Musk was forced to buy the thing for $44 billion – the worst deal I ever heard of – he begged me to come back. Begged. He would have gone down on his knees, believe me. But I don't want to help Elon Musk. I can't stand the guy. He looks like a frog that thinks it's smarter than all the other frogs. And he says he's richer than me. How could some pasty nerd with a hair transplant be the world's richest man?

Elon acts like some kind of genius, but his rockets blow up and his dumb electric cars catch fire. Total fraud. He's always been jealous of Trump, because I sleep with thousands of beautiful women and the best he can do is Grimes, who looks like she doesn't shower. Now he's supporting Virgin Ron DeSantis. Go figure. I'm sure little Elon would love to run for president himself. But he can't, because – just like Obama – he was born in Africa.

I was still jonesing for posts on my way to the laundry. Which may be why I stopped paying attention and walked straight into another inmate. Now, I'm a big guy – six foot three, some would say six foot four. But I barely came up to this freak's belly button. He was heavyset, with red hair and pale, freckled skin. He looked down at me, his eyes completely blank. I won't say I was scared. Still, I was very aware this guy could tear my spine out my back without breaking a sweat.

'Whoa, big fella,' I said, turning on the charm. 'I didn't see you there. No hard feelings?'

He kept staring. Then, without a word, he walked on, causing the jail to shake with every footstep. I breathed a sigh of relief.

'Mr Trump! I see you're making friends.'

Clint, captain of the guards, came up to me. All smiles. Probably angling for more autographs.

'Who's the lunk?' I asked.

'Oh, that's Kong. He's harmless. Except for all the people he harms.'

'What's he in for?'

'Homicide. I heard he ripped a guy's arms off and beat him to death with them.'

This didn't exactly put me at ease. I happen to be very attached to my arms, which are fabulous.

Things got worse when I finished my shift in the laundry. I was shuffling out, limbs aching, when a couple of cons blocked my way. I turned and saw two more behind me. They had shaved heads, neck tattoos, the whole nine yards. These were nasty guys. Real bad *hombres*. One of them stepped forward. I pride myself on being able to size up who's in charge in any given situation. This was clearly the leader.

'Well, well, well,' he said, 'if it isn't Mr Big Shot. The commander-in-chief himself.'

'That's right,' I said. I knew I had to act tough. I am tough, but I also had to act it. 'Who the hell are you?'

'Folks in here call me Shank.'

'Why do they call you that?'

'My full name's Carl Shankowitz. Also, I shank people.'

I'd been in jail long enough to know this meant stab with an improvized weapon. A sharpened spoon or toothbrush, something like that. Suffice it to say, I wasn't looking to get shanked. No thank you. Still, I couldn't back down. It's like in business – you let someone dominate you once, they'll do it every time.

'Well, if you're going to stab me, you better stab me,' I said. 'At least I wouldn't have to smell your rotten breath anymore.'

There was a long, horrible pause. Then Shank burst out laughing. His goons followed suit.

'Rotten breath, I love that,' he said, wiping his eyes. Then he grabbed me and put his lips to my ear.

'You better watch yourself, Mr President,' he hissed. 'You may be a fat old man, but fellas in here ain't discriminating. If you're not careful, someone might just grab you by the pussy.'

I wasn't sure what he meant by this, but I didn't like the sound of it. I pushed past

Shank and his boys, ignoring their very nasty comments. They let me go, but I'd be lying if I said I got much sleep last night. It's clear that to survive in this place you need someone who has your back. So I'm going to do something I've never done before. I'm going to make a friend.

DAY ELEVEN

I made a friend! It was on my first attempt, which is most likely a record. I shouldn't be surprised, given how likable I am. What happened was this – I stood in the yard, sizing up the other cons, looking for a potential buddy. None of them seemed like suitable candidates. There were meth heads with sunken eyes, twitchy psychos talking to themselves, gang members covered head to toe in tattoos. There was that giant Kong, occupying a whole bench by himself and staring straight at a wall. Not promising.

Then, finally, I saw a guy sitting alone on the bleachers. He had a slight build, mousy hair and glasses. I could tell from one glance that this was a high-class guy. White collar. Presumably he sat on his own because he wasn't a scumbag like everybody else here. I went over and shook his hand.

'Donald J. Trump, CEO of the Trump Organization, host of *The Apprentice* and 45th President of the United States.'

'Of course,' he said. 'I'm Larry. Larry Pryzbylewski.'

Turns out Larry was in finance before he came here. Worked on Wall Street during the eighties. We reminisced about long work lunches, wearing suspenders and being able to flirt with our secretaries before all this #MeToo crap. We hit it off immediately. Larry's smart, easygoing and – most importantly – thinks I'm a genius business titan. I didn't ask why he'd been locked up. Probably some made-up bullshit, like with me.

Anyway, it doesn't matter. Trump is a great judge of character. Apart from the people I've been close to that went on to betray me – Mike Pence, Chris Christie, Omarosa, Anthony Scaramucci and many, many others. But Larry isn't like that. I can tell he's one hundred percent on the level. I think ours will be a long and fruitful friendship.

DAY TWELVE

Sat down for lunch with Larry, my new best buddy. I've traditionally been a lone wolf, but now I was starting to see the point of friends.* Having a pal to share my trials with made them more bearable. The only thing it didn't improve was the food. Today we were allegedly served lasagna, but it was more like grayish glop. I pushed it around my plate, taking a reluctant bite every couple of minutes. Larry, on the other hand, wolfed it down.

'Yum, yum,' he said. 'I may try and get a second helping.'

I frowned.

'Larry, this stuff tastes like ass. Why would you go back for more?'

'Oh, I'll eat anything.'

With that, my buddy returned to the line. A beat later, Clint the guard waddled up.

'Mr Trump! How's it hanging?'

'It's hanging very beautifully. And very low. I have no problems in that department, believe me.'

'Glad to hear it.'

He glanced over at the line for food where Larry stood.

'I couldn't help but notice you're spending time with Prisoner Pryzbylewski,' he said, a

---

* As in companions, not the NBC sitcom. That show was totally overrated. Chandler – not funny! Mean! And Jennifer Aniston is a real piece of work. I tried to take her furniture shopping in the nineties. Tell you the truth, I moved on her like a bitch and she turned me down. Her loss.

little nervous. 'Just thought I should warn you, he can get . . . bitey.'

'Bitey? What do you mean bitey?'

'I mean he bites. The guy seems meek, but if you're not careful, he's liable to take a chunk out of you. I guess that's not a surprise, given what he's in here for.'

I was starting to get a bad feeling in my stomach. And not just because of the lasagna.

'What did Larry do?'

'He's a cannibal. Killed and ate six people. Papers said he was like Hannibal Lecter without the fava beans or the accent.'

I had spent half an hour forcing down glop. Now it threatened to come back up.

'Anyway, you guys have fun together,' said Clint, cheery again. 'Just watch your back. And your neck. And your ears, your fingers . . . Anything that could be bitten, really.'

The human thumb waddled off. I was still reeling from this new information when Larry sat back down beside me, a mountain of glop on his tray.

'You know,' he said, 'if we ever get out of this place, I'd love to have you for dinner.'

I told him he was a very nasty freak and left. I mean, Jesus Christ, a cannibal? That's disgusting. I could never eat a person – I only eat processed food. Of course, as a billionaire, I have often been invited to private islands where human flesh is consumed. But, as with Epstein, I always took a raincheck.

Anyway, this goes to show why you should never engage with people.

DAY THIRTEEN

Still no visitors other than my dipshit son. Has anyone been treated as unfairly as Trump? Part of me worries that a lifetime of treating people as objects and relationships as transactional has left me isolated. Then I remember that, no, everybody loves me.

DAY FOURTEEN

I sat on the bleachers in the yard, feeling sorry for myself. I have the best personality, I thought, so why can't I find a friend who's not a nut job? Then I heard a deep, rich voice with a soft, southern twang. It said: 'Hello there. I believe you're new at Smallhand.'

I looked up to see a good-looking African-American, middle-aged, with salt-and-pepper hair.

'I'm hardly new,' I said. 'I've been here two weeks.'

He smiled a wise African-American smile.

'Well, you're new compared to me. I've been here thirty years.'

He held out his hand. I'm a germaphobe, so usually I do my best to avoid handshakes. For some reason, I felt I could trust this guy. I shook.

'The name on my rap sheet is Boyd Jackson,' he said, 'but folks round here call me Orange.'

'Why's that?'

'On account of my affection for the juice. Being from Orange County, Florida, it's all I drank growing up.'

Boyd reminded me of someone, but I couldn't remember who. Which is strange, because I have an amazing memory, unlike Biden, who we call Dementia Joe.

I said, 'I'm President Donald J. Trump.'

'I know who you are, sir. Matter of fact, I admire you greatly.'

'Of course you do. The blacks love Trump.'

'We do. And we don't mind being called "the blacks". We like it, actually.'

I nodded with great force.

'This is what I've been saying. I'm the least racist guy you'll ever meet.'

'Yes indeed. And woke Democrats are the real racists. Everyone knows Trump is best for minorities. If felons could vote, I'd have voted for you twice.'

It was great to meet a freethinking ethnic

who coincidentally agreed with all of my opinions. Suddenly, I realized who he reminded me of.

'Hey, you look exactly like the Oscar-winning actor Morgan Freeman.'

He laughed, his brown eyes twinkling.

'So people tell me.'

'And you sound just like him.'

'They tell me that too. Now, sir, you may be wondering why I approached you. Truth is, I've been looking for a buddy in here for years. I would be honored to spend time with Donald Trump, our greatest ever president.'

This was exactly what I wanted to hear. Still, I played it cool. If there's one thing you learn in business, it's to never seem desperate.

'What's in it for me?' I asked.

He smiled again. His resemblance to Morgan Freeman in that one movie was uncanny.

'You're a very stable genius,' he said, 'and I would never presume to teach you anything. But maybe I could share some tips on prison life – give you the benefit of my experience.'

I stood up and placed a normal-sized hand on his shoulder.

'Orange, I think this is the start of a beautiful friendship.'

'I think so too, sir.'

'You know what? Forget about the "sir" crap. Just call me Don.'

'Sure thing, Don.'

I wrinkled my nose.

'Actually, that feels wrong. You should call me sir.'

'That's fine by me, sir.'

For the rest of exercise period, we talked about my tremendous achievements and how Barack Obama was an illegitimate president born in Kenya. I've always thought that friendship is for women and gays, but it felt good to make a human connection. Orange is a wonderful human being and I think spending time with him will help me get through this. Plus, he's African-American, so when people call me racist, I can tell them I have a black best friend. Checkmate!

4

Psycho Therapy

DAY FIFTEEN

Had a meeting with my attorney, Lionel McGill.
This guy's a killer, the best in the business.
He's so good that none of the top firms will hire
him in case he makes them look bad. I only hire
the best people. And people who don't complain
when I stiff them.

I arrived in the visiting room feeling positive.
McGill wore a lime-green suit, sky-blue shirt
and orange tie. I could smell his cologne
through the Plexiglas screen. They say I use
fake tan, but his face looked like mahogany.
The guy's a class act. He greeted me with
finger-guns.

'Donny, baby! By which I mean Mr
President, no disrespect.'

'Lionel. How's the appeal going?'

'It's going gangbusters. I still need to cross
some i's, dot some t's. But once I submit, you'll
be out of here in no time.'

'So you're confident? Because the judge said
the evidence against me was overwhelming.'

He waved a dismissive hand.

'It's in the bag, my word as a McGill. You can consider that conviction overturned.'

This was music to my ears. Good music, like they'd play at one of my rallies. 'Macho Man', 'Tiny Dancer', something like that.

Just then, I realized that McGill's lime-green suit was all wrinkled up. There were also coffee stains on his lapels. At least, I hope they were coffee stains. I asked him about it and he said, 'Oh, that's nothing. I've been sleeping in my car. So I can get to my clients as soon as they need me. Not because I can't afford a home.'

I was immediately reassured. With a lawyer that dedicated, I would be out in no time. I changed the subject to the Republican presidential primaries. I asked, 'How's my campaign doing?'

'It's doing beautiful,' he said. 'It's doing great.'

'Oh yeah? What am I on? Fifty percent? Sixty?'

'Two.'

'Sixty-two percent?'

'No, two percent.'

'What the hell? That's not great at all.'

'Yeah, it seems even the Republican party has a line they won't cross, and that's voting for convicted felons. But I wouldn't worry. They'll come round, or my name's not Eduardo Rodriguez.'

'What? I thought your name was Lionel McGill.'

'Right. Is that not what I said? I'm pretty sure that's what I said.'

Weird guy, but one hell of a lawyer. I asked him to check in on Melania, nudge her about a visit. It's weird she hasn't come to see me yet. Surely she misses her wonderful, very faithful husband. I guess she must just be afraid of prisons. Maybe it's a superstition – some crazy Eastern European thing.

Had another good talk with Orange during exercise period. We watched as some cons were shooting hoops. He agreed that I could have joined the NBA if I'd wanted to. And that I would have been the greatest white player in basketball history. Maybe even up there with Jordan, LeBron and Kareem Abdul-Jabbar. I considered showing him my 360-degree, one-handed slam dunk, but I didn't want to embarrass the guys who were playing. Modesty is so important.

DAY SIXTEEN

Today I had an assessment with the shrink here at Smallhand. I've never seen a psychiatrist before – why would I spend all that money when I'm totally sane? I'm the most sane of anyone, believe me. Tremendously sane. People say to me, 'Sir, I wish I had your sanity.' But the choice was between seeing a shrink and staying in my cell, so I saw the shrink.

Upon entering the office, I was surprised to find a well-dressed brunette in her late forties, with glasses and a wry smile. She sat in one of two chairs in a poky little room, writing in a notepad.

'Mr Trump,' she said, 'please take a seat.'

Her voice was smoky and provocative. I usually prefer blondes, and anyone over thirty-five is pushing it, but she looked good to me. Maybe I've been surrounded by guys for too long. As I sat opposite her, I felt Little Donald move. Not that Little Donald is little. He's very impressive, no matter what Stormy Daniels says. And anyway, she's a porn star, so she's used to unrealistic schlongs.

'Good morning,' said the sexy psychologist, 'I'm Dr Conti.'

'Conti?' I said. 'What is that, Italian?'
She nodded.

'My ancestors were from Caserta.'

'I love Italians. Working in New York real estate, I knew a lot of them. Y'know, mafia types. Those were scary guys. Though, actually, they were scared of me.'

I thought this might get her excited. Instead, she pursed her lips.

'I can assure you, none of my relatives are involved in organized crime.'

'Whatever you need to tell yourself, sweetheart.'

'Dr Conti.'

'Dr Conti, sweetheart.'

It's a funny thing. Here was an educated feminist, a member of the coastal elite. Just the kind of person the mainstream media will tell you hates Trump. And yet she obviously had the hots for me. I hit her with my most seductive smile. Many have said my teeth are my best feature. They're very white – blinding, in fact – and definitely not dentures.

For the rest of the hour, I put the moves on her using my words, which are the best words. Women say I have a silver tongue, but I would never settle for silver. I have a gold tongue, 24-carat. I flirted and made clever quips, like James Bond would. Clearly, they had the intended effect – at the end of our session, Conti asked if I could see her on a weekly basis. Apparently, I'm a 'fascinating case study in narcissism'. Yeah right, honey. She says she wants to get inside my head. I say she wants to get inside my pants.

Lying in my bed after lights out, I thought about Dr Conti long and hard. It's ironic that she's a shrink when she makes a certain part of me grow.

REPORT ON PRISONER #42069

By Dr Jane Conti, M.D.

Resident Psychologist, Smallhand State Prison

During our initial meeting, the subject demonstrated a mixture of arrogance, cruelty and solipsism. Perhaps most striking is his complete incuriosity toward anything but himself. I had often wondered whether his public persona is an act, concealing a more nuanced and conflicted figure. Based on first impressions, it is not. He also made a series of boorish statements that he seemed to believe were subtle and suave.

While the subject displays an obvious (and highly distasteful) attraction to me, I am inclined to continue our sessions. On the surface, he is a classic sociopath: manipulative, deceptive, convinced of his own superiority and indifferent to right and wrong. However, even in our short time together, I fancy I detected flashes of recognizable human emotion. I believe a breakthrough is possible, and would be of great value both to the patient and the field of psychiatry. For all his defense mechanisms and layers of learned behavior, there might – just might – be more to Donald Trump.

5

Shanks for Nothing

DAY TWENTY-ONE

The guards clanged on my bars and told me I
had a visitor. Assuming it was Don Jr again,
I dragged my heels all the way to the visiting
room. But it wasn't DJTJ. It was the gorgeous
and very fashionable Melania, my third – and
potentially final – wife.

Even behind the smudged glass, she looked
radiant. Which surprised me. I thought she
would look haggard, washed out, bags under her
eyes. After all, it was three weeks since she'd
seen her beloved hubby. Three weeks without
kisses, touches or Little Donald. But she seemed
to be handling the situation well. In fact, she
looked happier than I'd seen her in years.

'Donult,' she said in that hot Slovenian
accent, 'I hope you are heving nice time in
preeson.'

'I don't know about nice,' I said, 'but I'm
keeping busy. You probably noticed how swole
I've gotten.'

Her face stayed blank, but I knew she was
turned on. That's what Slavs are like – they

keep everything close to the chest. Also close to Melania's chest were her boobs, which looked phenomenal.

'By the way,' I said, 'being in here hasn't dampened my masculine urges. Maybe the next time I see you, it could be a conjugal visit.'

She trembled with excitement. It was definitely a tremble, not a shudder, believe me.

'Yes, maybe ve could do zat . . .'

'And y'know, once my conviction's overturned, we'll be able to make sex every night. In all three positions . . .'

I waggled my eyebrows suggestively. Melania wasn't looking quite so radiant now. In fact, she looked kind of green.

'Yep,' I continued, 'I'll be out of here any day now. McGill's working round the clock and he's the best in the business. Trump has the greatest people.'

She drummed her fingers, not quite meeting my eye.

'I'm gled you are okay, Donult. Now I must go. I buy new clothes for Barron – he grow another foot this month.'

As Melania walked away, I finally realized why it had taken her so long to visit. She knew that the moment she saw me, she would be overcome with desire. Even through a partition, my pheromones are irresistible. It must have taken all her willpower not to throw herself at the Plexiglas, like a bird attacking its own reflection. I guess she thought it would be less painful to stay away completely than remind herself of what she's missing.

DAY TWENTY-FOUR

Orange and I were in the yard, ranking every season of *The Apprentice* from great to magnificent, when I heard a wolf whistle.

'Heeeeey, Trumpy Trumpy!'

I turned to see Shank and his gang strut up.

'Damn, Donald,' he said, 'you look like shit.'

It's true I don't look my best right now. I have a very distinctive appearance, one that takes a team of stylists to maintain. And they don't let you have stylists in jail. As a result, my skin has lost its healthy orange glow, and my hair hangs down in strands, exposing what a dumb person might mistake for baldness. Man, I miss that hair-helmet.

'Check out his face!' Shank continued. 'It's the same color as his hands. He looks like one of those fish that live in a cave.'

I'd been trying to keep my head down, but I'm a counterpuncher. When you come at Trump, he hits back twenty times as hard.

'You know what, Shank? You're a very nasty guy. No class. You would never get invited to the *Vanity Fair* Oscar Party.'

Shank leapt forwards, grabbing my collar and slamming me against the brick wall. He pulled a sharpened toothbrush out of his sleeve and held it to my neck.

'The fuck you just say to me, bitch?'

Obviously, I could have beaten the hell out of him if I wanted to. People don't know this, but I'm an expert in the Israeli martial art of Krav Maga. I even created an American version called Krav MAGA. But I didn't want to get punished for breaking every bone in the guy's body. Instead, I tactically decided to cry and wet myself, to lull him into a false sense of security.

'I'm sorry,' I said. 'I'm sorry, I'm sorry, I'm sorry.'

My gambit worked. Shank totally bought that I was a coward. He screamed in my face, his breath very disgusting.

'Say I would get invited to the *Vanity Fair* Oscar Party!'

'You would get invited to the *Vanity Fair* Oscar Party! You'd be the guest of honor!'

Shank let out a grunt and threw me to the ground. To maintain the illusion of me not being macho, I curled up in a ball and did a high-pitched wail.

'Come on,' Shank said to his boys. 'The sight of this pussy is making me sick.'

Once they were gone, I got to my feet and dusted myself off.

'Sir, are you okay?' asked Orange.

I glared at him.

'No thanks to you, pal. You didn't lift a finger to help.'

'I wanted to, sir, but it would only have made things worse. Guys like that are looking for a fight.'

'We'll settle this later,' I said, in a very tough, very dignified way. Then I went inside to change my soiled jumpsuit.

DAY TWENTY-FIVE

I was in my cell, exhausted after a brutal shift in the laundry. I lay on my cot, daydreaming about the very beautiful Miss Kim Basinger, who I totally could have had in the eighties. Then – CLANG! – one of the guards hit my bars with his baton.

'Trump, visitor for you.'

I got up as fast as I could (one minute, two minutes tops). Who could it be? A member of my adoring family? Or one of my glamorous celebrity friends, like Jon Voight or Kid Rock? So talented.

What I saw in the visiting room was a nasty surprise, let me tell you. A nasty surprise and a nasty woman. Behind the screen sat an older blonde in a hideous pantsuit. It was none other than Crooked Hillary Clinton.

'Hello, Donald,' she said, with a big, fake smile.

'Actually,' I said, 'you're meant to call me Mr President. I'd do the same, except you never became president, did you?'

She looked like she'd swallowed a wasp. A live one. Then out came the smile again.

'I followed your trial very closely, Donald. It was the most fun I've had since you got Covid. When you were sent to jail, I knew I'd have to see for myself. And hey, orange suits you!'

I did my standard tough-guy pout. Hillary always got under my skin, but I was determined not to show it. She continued in her grating robot voice.

'Remember that chant at your rallies? *Lock her up! Lock her up!* Isn't it funny how things turn out?'

I had spent the afternoon scrubbing skid marks off gangbangers' briefs. This was the last thing I needed. So I decided to fight back.

'Well, thanks for visiting,' I said. 'Where's your horny psycho of a husband?'

Crooked clenched her jaw.

'Bill's back home in Chappaqua. He doesn't send his best.'

'Are you sure you should be here? What if he gets in another situation with an intern?'

She was acting casual, but I could tell she was pissed. I have, like, a sixth sense when it comes to bullying.

'I trust my husband,' she said. 'Unlike you, I don't just see the worst in people.'

'I see people as they are. For instance, you're Crooked Hillary.'

She rolled her eyes.

'I must say, Donald, I've grown rather tired of that moniker.'

'Not the first Monica you've had problems with.'

She took a deep breath, trying to control her temper.

'Very nice. You've always been good at insults. But they don't change the most important fact.'

'Which is?'

'Tonight I'll be sleeping in my own bed, and you'll be here.'

I didn't have an answer to this. After another fifteen minutes of trading barbs, Hillary left. The sad thing is, I kind of wish she'd stayed longer. We may hate each other, but it's better than being alone.

6

I Beg Your Pardon

DAY THIRTY

So I just got out of the infirmary. Here's what
happened. I was headed to my shift in the
laundry when a couple of guys popped up and
pulled me into a stairwell. Suddenly I was face-
to-ugly-face with Shank.

'What the hell are you doing?' I said, very
toughly.

'I wanted to show you something. See, when
you've been locked up as long as I have, you get
to know a place. You learn funny little details.
For instance, between this landing and the
basement, there are exactly one hundred fifteen
steps.'

With a vicious smile, he gestured to an object
beside him. It was one of the barrels from the
laundry.

'You're going on a flight, Mr President, and
here's your ride. Let's call it Stair Force One.'

They stuffed me inside the barrel and rolled
it down the staircase. I bounced three or four
times before going unconscious.

Eventually one of the guards found me and I

was taken to the prison doctor. He checked me out, then gave me the results.

'The good news is your injuries are superficial and there's no concussion. The bad news is your overall health is terrible.'

I told him this couldn't be accurate. The White House doctor called Trump the greatest physical specimen in history. Who am I going to believe, the Physician to the President or some jailhouse quack?

'Nonetheless,' he said, 'you need to lose weight. No more pudding cups in the mess hall.'

Unbelievable. One of the only pleasures I have left, and the so-called experts want to take it away. This is why I don't listen to medical types. They're always feeding you bullshit, like saying exercise is good for you, or you shouldn't inject bleach to cure Covid.

DAY THIRTY-TWO

Another horrible, unfair day. I got a visit from my lawyer, McGill, who wore an eggplant suit, canary-yellow shirt and pink paisley-pattern tie. Honestly, the guy didn't look so hot – he had a black eye and hadn't shaved in a few days. Still, I was happy to see my legal eagle. The best attorney in the tristate area. Then he told me the appeal to overturn my conviction had been denied.

'WHAT?' I yelled. He let out a yawn.

'Sorry, I haven't slept in seventy-two hours. I'm operating on Red Bull and vodka right now. But yeah, the appeal's dead. Finito. Done-zo.'

'You told me it was in the bag. How did this happen?'

McGill shrugged. 'I guess cos of all the evidence against you? That's generally a problem, legally speaking.'

'Okay, we appeal again. Appeal harder.'

'No can do. That's the other thing I wanted to tell you – you're gonna need a new lawyer.'

'Why? Because I never pay my bills?'

'No, because I'm being prosecuted myself. I need to focus on my defense.'

My jaw fell open. 'Prosecuted? For what?'

'Fraud, embezzlement, obstruction of justice, drunk driving – you name it, I've done it. Actually, I shouldn't admit that . . .'

By now my head was in my hands. How had I been taken in by this ambulance chaser?

'When I hired you, you said you were this hotshot lawyer – the best in the business.'

'With all due respect, I never said that. You decided I was great because you liked my haircut.'

Unbelievable. Does anyone have worse luck than Trump? Any time I trust a person, they turn out to be a traitor, a grifter or a crook. It's like there's something about me that attracts dirtballs. I'll never understand it.

DAY THIRTY-THREE

After a night of stewing over my talk with McGill, I made a decision. Desperate times call for desperate measures. I was going to call the fake current president, Joe Biden.

Let me tell you about Joe Biden – Sleepy Joe, we call him. Quite frankly, the guy's a mess. He's in his early eighties – wrinkled, senile, nearly dead. Not like me. I'm in my late seventies – powerful, virile, full of spunk. It's been said I have the most spunk anyone's ever had. Terrific spunk, believe me. Joe, he hasn't got any. Or if he does, it's made out of dust.

Sleepy Joe . . . He looks ridiculous, with his facelifts and his veneers. And his hair's horrible – wispy, see-through, fake. The guy clearly got plugs. You look at pictures of him in the seventies and he has a chrome dome. I say bald men should accept their condition. Trying to cover it up only makes them look worse. Fortunately, that's not something I have to worry about.

As physically decrepit as Joe is, he's much worse mentally. He can't go five minutes without flashing back to the 1960s. He tells these long, rambling stories that go nowhere and probably didn't happen. I still can't believe I lost an election to that Alzheimer's case. Except I didn't lose – it was stolen. People were allowed to vote who never should have been (Democrats).

Anyway, I decided I would get in touch. You see, there's this little-known rule that any former president can call the sitting president at any time, and they have to pick up. So, standing at Smallhand's bank of payphones, trying to shut out the yelling in the background, I dialed the number for the Oval Office. Sure enough, Biden picked up. I barely had time to say hello before he launched into one of his endless anecdotes.

'Listen, Mac, when I was a kid in Scranton, we used to eat flapjacks every day. We'd go to Auntie Mavis's Flapjack Emporium. And, God bless her, Mavis made the smallest flapjacks you've ever seen. But she wasn't trying to flimflam us – she wasn't a bad gal – it's just every flapjack she made came out the size of a postage stamp. So me and a couple buddies, Popcorn and the Professor, we—'

'Joe, I'm gonna have to stop you there – I only have ten minutes. I wanted to ask a favor.'

'A favor? From me?'

'This whole prison situation isn't working out. So I was hoping you could give me a pardon. Y'know, like Ford pardoned Nixon. Can you do me a solid, president to president?'

There was a long pause. Too long. I worried that Joe had forgotten about the call and wandered off. Then he spoke.

'I don't know, Donald . . . You've said some unacceptable things. Like I've got a few screws loose in the . . . in the cuckoo clock. Or that my beautiful boy Hunter . . . that he did bad laptop stuff. Yeah, he's made mistakes, but he's only fifty-three years old.'

'Look, I'm sorry for anything I may have said about you or your crackhead son. Forgive me?'

'Sorry won't cut it. I want you to beg.'

'Okay, I beg, I beg. I hereby officially beg. Is that good enough?'

'Not quite. You gotta admit I won the 2020 election fair and . . . fair and . . . y'know, the shape.'

'Fine, I admit it,' I said, with my long, thick, manly fingers crossed.

'Hot dog! I haven't felt this triumphant since my team won the All-Scranton Little League trophy. This was back in 1955, and everyone was listening to Sammy Sarsaparilla and the Gigolos. What a band! They—'

'Yeah, fantastic. So you'll pardon me?'

'Sure thing, Don. To be honest, I can't remember why we locked you up in the first place.'

I thought: You barely remember anything from the past twenty years. But I kept my mouth shut. I was overcome with relief. And, to tell the truth, I felt grateful to the old geezer. Then I realized he was still mumbling some bullshit.

'Y'know, I always believed in second chances. Maybe it's cos I'm Irish. My great-aunt Gertrude, she used to say to me: Joey—'

At this point I hung up. I was grateful, but not grateful enough to listen to his crap.

Walking back to my cell, I felt great, like I'd just sealed the deal on a casino in Atlantic City, or got Cindy Crawford's phone number. I was close to freedom, so close I could smell it (along with the usual prison smells of vomit, body odor and disinfectant). My long nightmare would soon be over.

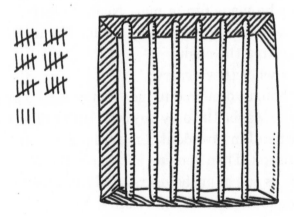

7

Biden His Time

DAY THIRTY-FIVE

Tossed a baseball around with Orange in the yard.

'Y'know, once I'm a free man, I can run for president again,' I said. 'After four years of Sleepy Joe, I'll be guaranteed to win in a landslide. That's despite the rigged system.'

'No doubt, sir,' he said, Morgan Freemanishly.

'And once I'm back in the Oval Office, it's no more Mr Nice Guy. The people who sent me here? Straight to jail. See how they like it. My political opponents? Jail. All the late-night hosts who made fun of me – Noah, Colbert, Meyers? Jail if they're lucky. As for Kimmel, he's getting the chair.'

'It's what they deserve.'

A thought occurred to me. 'You're a good guy, Orange. Maybe the only guy who isn't unfair to me. When I'm president, I'm gonna give you a full pardon. Then you can join me in the White House as one of my advisers. And together, we can Make America Great Again – Again.'

My buddy wiped a tear from his eye.

'Sir, your generosity is exceeded only by your wisdom. I don't deserve your friendship. You are the greatest human being who has ever lived, and that includes Jesus Christ.'

Hey, when he's right, he's right.

DAY FORTY-TWO

Still nothing from our senile commander-in-chief. I'm not worried, though. I know better than anyone how busy the president can be. You have to watch eight hours of cable TV a day, play frequent rounds of golf and send hundreds of tweets to celebrities who piss you off. That is, if you're good at the job.

Anyway, Sleepy Joe will get round to pardoning me. He has to. We made a deal. Now, personally, I've gone back on a lot of deals. But no way is Biden smart enough to do that.

DAY FIFTY-FOUR

It's been weeks without a word from Sleepy. I'm famous for my emotional control, but I'm starting to go a bit nuts. Life in this place is unbearable, truly. Even after the barrel stunt, Shank is still on my case. This morning, he knocked the tray out of my hands in the mess hall.

'One of these days,' he said, 'I'm gonna stick you like the pig you are.'

'Yeah, well,' I said, 'pigs are actually very smart, maybe the smartest of any mammal, and they're being recognized more and more. So thanks for admitting I'm smarter than you.'

Shank responded by drawing a finger across his neck. 'One of these days, piggy. One of these days.'

He went over and sat with his gang, who all started oinking at me. Very threatening oinks. I don't understand what this guy's problem is. How could anybody hate Trump? He must be getting paid by my enemies – the DNC, CNN, PB&J, R2-D2 . . .

DAY FIFTY-EIGHT

Had another session with the lovely Dr Conti. Seeing her is always the highlight of my week. I get to flirt and steal glances at the very nice figure beneath her business suit. In exchange, I have to play along with all the psychiatric shit – Daddy didn't love me, my pet goldfish died, blah blah blah. Of course, none of that stuff affects me. But I act like it does for her benefit. On this occasion, I shed a single, very masculine, tear. Liberal women love it when a man cries – I could tell my cheek wasn't the only thing getting wet.

NOTES ON SESSION WITH PRISONER #42069

By Dr Jane Conti, M.D.

After weeks of consultations, I believe we are finally beginning to make progress. Though couched in his customary bluster and bravado, the subject has started to admit some vulnerability. During our latest session, he broke down in floods of tears, his whole body racked with sobs. For all the damage he has inflicted upon this country, I couldn't help but sympathize. Despite being in his late seventies, he often comes across like a little boy.

The subject describes himself as 'rock solid in terms of psychological', which is far from the truth. He evidently suffers from childhood trauma, in particular a lack of affection from his domineering businessman father. While he initially displayed no capacity for self-reflection, it has become clear that he bears a great deal of guilt and regret, albeit buried beneath layers of braggadocio.

It is my fervent hope that the subject can be rehabilitated. He has done so much to derange America. Imagine the good that could come from fixing his damaged psyche.

DAY SIXTY-FOUR

The thing I've been waiting for finally happened – a visit from Ivanka, my bombshell of a daughter. I can tell you, she was a sight for sore eyes. That long blonde hair. Those full, rose-colored lips. And that voluptuous body, all six feet of it. I only wish the Plexiglas hadn't been there, so I could have kissed her and sat her on my lap. Instead, I had to settle for talking through a phone.

I told her about my time at Smallhand, and how all the other prisoners respect me and, in fact, are scared of me. But something was up. She frowned and stared at her Manolo Blahniks throughout. It was like she didn't want to make eye contact.

'Sweetie, what's the matter?' I asked. 'You're way too pretty not to smile.'

She gave me a guilty – but still very alluring – look.

'Dad, this is difficult to say . . . I won't be visiting you again.'

'Huh? Why the hell not?'

'I need to put distance between us. I'm relaunching my clothing line and I don't want you associated with the brand.'

I couldn't believe what I was hearing.

'But I'm great for brands! People think of Trump, they think luxury, prestigious, elite!'

She shook her gorgeous head. 'That's not how it works anymore. Nowadays the money is in woke capitalism. Consumers want to feel like buying a product makes them a better person – progressive, inclusive, an ally. And the fact is, you represent the opposite of all that. You're toxic. In terms of image, I mean . . .'

I was getting desperate. I started bargaining. 'Honey, if you need me to be woke, I can be woke. I'll do social justice like you wouldn't believe.'

'Dad, I don't give a shit about social justice. All I care about is money. And you're getting in the way of me making it.'

'Ivanka, baby, I—'

'Sorry, Daddy. Take care of yourself, okay?'

She hung up and left, which gave me a good view of her getaway sticks. I sat alone for a while, feeling conflicted. On the one hand, it hurt to be rejected by my hottest child. On the other, I was proud of her for putting business above family. A chip off the old block.

DAY SEVENTY

I finally broke and called Old Man Biden again.

'Hey there, Don, thanks for checking in. I was just thinking about the time I took Betsy Haddock to the state fair. The year was 1962 and I was making a clean living selling bees door to door. Trouble is, you had to put the hive in a wheelbarrow and—'

'Joe,' I interrupted, 'what the hell's going on with my pardon?'

'Pardon?'

'Yeah, my pardon.'

'No, I mean pardon as in . . . what?'

I scowled so hard my face hurt. But I kept my tone as sweet as I could.

'We agreed several weeks ago that you would grant me a full presidential pardon for any crimes I may have committed.'

'Don, I have no idea what you're talking about. Now I'm Irish, so I like a tall tale as much as the next Jack. But a pardon? After what you did? That sounds like malarkey to me.'

I've been told my temper is the best, better than many monks. At this point, though, something snapped.

'Are you fucking senile? Or are you fucking with me because I call you senile?'

Joe chuckled, almost like he was enjoying himself.

'C'mon, man, don't be sour. Hey, I know what might cheer you up. I've got someone here you'll want to talk to.'

I listened to Joe shuffle across the Oval Office carpet and creakily pass the phone. My stomach dropped when I heard a familiar voice.

'Hello, Donald,' said Crooked Hillary Clinton. 'I'm so glad you called. I just got some news I'm dying to share. Joe has named me his Special Adviser on Presidential Pardons. Do you know what that means?'

I could guess, but I didn't want to give her the pleasure.

'It means I have the power of veto over any pardon the president might consider. By the way,' she said, 'how's your cell? I hope it's comfortable, because you'll be spending the rest of your life in it.'

'Such a nasty woman!' I shouted. 'Oh, and, honey? Those pantsuits are disgusting. Why don't you use some of your dirty money to hire a personal shopper?'

I slammed the phone back in its cradle.

That night was the roughest I've had here since my first. The years stretched out in front of me. Sure, I'm in fantastic physical condition. But the fact remains, I'm middle-aged. Maybe even late-middle-aged. I don't have time to waste. There are still so many things I want to achieve. Such as . . .

1. Adding my head to Mount Rushmore

Now, maybe the people of South Dakota don't want a fifth president up there. That's fine. We can just get rid of Teddy Roosevelt. Honestly, who needs that four-eyed prick, with his walrus mustache? Trump is way more handsome. I have a great head. Tremendous head.

2. Building a Trump Tower on Mars

The Red Planet has a lot of development potential. Also, aliens need to see that the human race is elegant and sophisticated.

3. Finally breaking up Ivanka's marriage

Sorry, Jared, but my baby can do better. Much, much better.

8

Don Gone

DAY SEVENTY-ONE

It's become clear I need to take matters into
my own hands (which, again, are above average
size). If Sleepy and Crooked are going to deny
me the pardon I deserve, then I have to escape.
But how? I don't have time to chisel through
the wall of my cell with a rock hammer, so that
was out. None of my other ideas – for instance,
impersonating the warden's wife or building a
jetpack in the workshop – seemed right. Despite
my big, beautiful brain, I was stumped.

Then the perfect idea fell into my lap.
Warden Snook marched into the yard, guards
either side of him. He lifted up a bullhorn.

'Proverbs 14:23 – in all labor there is profit,
but idle chatter leads only to poverty. I am
offering you sinners a chance to profit from
your labor. I need twenty men for an outdoor
detail. You'll be cleaning the highway, one dollar
an hour.'

I volunteered immediately. Not because I
believe in the value of hard work or any of that
bullshit. No, I volunteered because it was a

chance to get out of Smallhand. My chances of escaping seem much better without barbed wire or twenty-foot walls.

I knew exactly what I would do once free – empty my secret bank accounts and flee the country. Maybe cross the border to Mexico (it's a problem when they come here, not the other way round). The beauty part is nobody would recognize me with human-colored skin or a hairstyle that doesn't require an architect. I'd be able to get to Zihuatanejo and live out my days as Donaldo Trumpez. Sure, I'd miss things from my old life. But I hear Mexico has McDonald's and Fox News, so I'd be all right. And some of the ladies down there are nearly as hot as Ivanka.

I told Orange about my plan. For once, he pushed back on me.

'Sir, in my thirty years at Smallhand, I've seen dozens of guys try to escape. None of them succeeded.'

'Yeah, because they were a bunch of dumb slobs. If they were as smart or physically fit as Trump, it would have gone different.'

He didn't look convinced. Which, if I can be completely honest, pissed me off. People have always underestimated Trump. They said I would never have a top-rated show on NBC. They said I would never win a presidential election. And they said my presidency would be a disaster, instead of what it was, a total triumph. So yes, it stings that Orange won't support me on this. But whatever he thinks, I'm one hundred percent confident my escape attempt will go according to plan.

DAY SEVENTY-THREE

Part One

My escape attempt didn't go according to plan. It was typical – I did everything right and I still got screwed!

First thing in the morning, me and the other cons were loaded on a prison bus and driven to the wetlands. The bus stopped on a stretch of highway surrounded by swamp. We were issued trash bags and pick-up tools, which we used to clear junk from the roadside. Fast food containers, used condoms, prosthetic limbs, that sort of thing. The whole time I was watching the guards, waiting for those low-IQ bozos to get distracted.

Sure enough, one rube pulled out his phone and started playing funny TikToks. The others crowded round, saying things like 'Gawsh, that cat sure is afraid of cucumbers' and 'That fella got hit in the balls, hyuck-yuck'. I took this as a cue to drop my items and shuffle away.

Once I reached the trees, I ran as fast as my legs would carry me (again, about two miles an hour).

Soon I found my path blocked by a pool of murky water. I dipped my foot in, but couldn't find the bottom. Clearly it was no go – I didn't want to drown or get eaten by a gator. If only someone had drained the swamp! Just then I heard a voice amplified by megaphone.

'Prisoner Trump, return to your work area immediately!'

I ran back through the trees, pushing my body to the limit, hitting maybe three miles an hour. Within minutes I was exhausted. Any man would have been, even an Olympic athlete. I doubled over, wheezing, dripping with sweat, close to fainting. Running was not an option – I had to hide. That's when I noticed it. Behind some ferns was an open drainage pipe.

It was small, but a big, well-built guy like me could just about fit inside . . .

I heard the sound of Dobermanns barking and guards trampling grass. My captors were getting close. I peered into the pipe. As a germaphobe, I obviously didn't love the idea of crawling through shit. Still, to get what you want, you sometimes have to do unpleasant things. Like when you're running for president, you have to visit Iowa. So I got down on my hands and knees. The tunnel was dark, stinking, horrible, but at the other end lay freedom. I took a deep breath and crawled inside.

I was a few feet in when I got stuck. Somehow my backside – which is very firm and tight for a guy my age – had become wedged. I tried to pull back, but I couldn't move an inch. It was unbelievable. What idiot designed this pipe? After a couple minutes of blind struggling, trying not to breathe through my nose, I heard the guards come up behind me. For a moment, there was silence. Then peals of laughter.

'Well, if it isn't President Fat-Ass!'

'Hail to the cheeks!'

'They should call you Donald Rump!'

After half an hour, I was yanked out of the pipe very roughly and put in chains. I won't say my escape attempt was a failure – Trump never fails. But I admit it wasn't my greatest success.

As soon as we got back to Smallhand, I was brought before Warden Snook. He acted mad, but I could tell he was loving it. He looked at me and made a big deal of wrinkling his nose.

'Prisoner #42069, you always reeked of sin. Now you reek of other things.'

It's true my uniform was covered in all kinds of shit. I smelled worse than Rudy Giuliani after one of his all-night steak-and-cigar binges. The warden continued.

'My men tell me they found you in a sewer. It's no surprise you would feel at home in such a place.'

'I'll tell you where I feel at home – the White House. And once I'm back there, I'm gonna lock you up. Lock you up in your own jail.'

Snook shook his head.

'There are none so blind as those who will not see.'

'Excuse me, I have perfect eyesight, okay? My vision is twenty-twenty, like the election that was stolen. Which, by the w—'

'I am speaking, Prisoner #42069, of delusion. Delusion and willful denial. You refuse to accept the reality of your situation, so let me make it plain. You are a disgraced figure. You are a convict, destined to die behind bars. And you are – to use a word of which you are excessively fond – a loser. You can reflect upon that during a week in solitary.'

'Fine,' I said, 'it'll be great to get away from the low-lives in this joint. One thing, though – can I shower first?'

The warden smirked, very nasty.

'No. I would have you reckon with the unholy stench of your corruption.'

He nodded to the guards.

'Son of a bitch!' I cried as I was dragged from his office. 'I'm gonna sue you for this. And then I'm gonna sue your god!'

9

Down in the Trumps

DAY SEVENTY-THREE

Part Two

The place they took me was called the Hole, so I didn't expect five-star accommodation. Still, I was disappointed. They shoved me inside a tiny stone room with no lighting. No anything, in fact – just a toilet without a seat. As I've said, when I'm alone too long I start thinking bad thoughts. To stave this off, I went through my mental list of people who've been unfair to me. Here's a brief extract:

- Robert Mueller
- Robert De Niro
- Nancy Pelosi
- Alec Baldwin (bad guy, bad impression)
- Democrats
- Republicans
- The Deep State
- Steve Bannon
- Morrissey

- Black Lives Matter thugs
- CHI-NA!
- Oscar the Grouch, who I wrote to, asking to appear on *Sesame Street* (he never replied)
- Cuomos Andrew and Chris
- Jimmies Fallon and Kimmel
- The people of Scotland
- Dr Fauci
- Hollywood
- The cast of *Hamilton*
- Megyn Kelly
- Whistleblowers
- John McCain
- All the states that didn't vote for me
- Co-lin Powell (it's pronounced 'Colin')
- Arnold Schwarzenegger
- Snoop Dogg
- Dogs in general
- Justin Trudeau
- Sir Isaac Newton
- McDonald's, for discontinuing their Big N' Tasty burger in 2011, leaving millions of fans devastated
- Pikachu, who I helped so much when he was starting out in showbiz

Thinking about the millions of slights I've suffered kept me occupied a while. It made me angry, and I like angry. But after a few days of bread and water, with no human interaction, I started having Bad Thoughts. I'm, like, a smart person. I have a very good brain. So how did I end up here? And why couldn't I get out? Maybe the Trump way of doing things wasn't always the greatest. Maybe Trump wasn't a noble genius who never did anything wrong. I know that sounds crazy, but solitary screws with your head.

Fortunately, this period of self-doubt didn't last long. One night – at least, I think it was night – it hit me. The problem wasn't that I'd been too Trump. I hadn't been Trump *enough*. So I came up with a plan. It's the best, brightest and, quite frankly, planniest plan ever. Nobody has plans like Trump.

Eventually I was let out, hosed off and taken back to Snook. He gave me one of his holier-than-thou smiles.

'So, Prisoner #42069, did you experience any epiphanies during your confinement?'

'No epiphanies. And I can say that for sure, because I know what the word means. But I did have a realization.'

'Oh?'

'I realize I've been very unfair to you. All you want is to help me and the other guys in here.'

His eyes lit up. 'Is that the prelude to a groveling apology?'

This was going to be tough – I've spent my life refusing to apologize. But, for my plan to work, I needed to fool him. So I used the same acting skills I displayed as Macaulay Culkin's scene partner in *Home Alone 2* (much better than the original).

'Warden Snook,' I said, 'I apologize from the bottom of my heart. Both for my misdeeds in here and the sins of my past life. I know I can never make up for the bad things I've done. All I ask is the chance to try.'

It goes without saying the guy bought it. He practically got hard at the idea of beating me.

'A week in the Hole does wonders for contrition. So am I to understand you've learned your lesson?'

'Absolutely. From now on, I'm gonna be a model prisoner. Not model like the women I date. Model as in good.'

'That is fine news.'

He got something out of a cabinet and handed it to me. It was a thick, leather-bound book with a gold cross on the front.

'What's this?' I said.

'The Holy Bible. For your further edification.'

'Thanks, Warden. I'm a huge fan of books written by Jesus.'

Of course, I had no intention of reading the thing. But it was pretty hefty. A useful weapon.

'Make good use of it,' said Snook.

'Oh, I will.'

I went out to the yard, staggering a little, blinded by the sun. Orange came up to me, looking concerned.

'Sir, are you okay? Solitary could break even the strongest man. By which I mean you.'

'I'm fine,' I said. 'In fact, I'm better than ever. Because I realized something in the Hole. I've been seeing things all wrong. What I'm going through right now isn't a punishment. It's an opportunity.'

'An opportunity?'

I nodded. 'I'm a brilliant tactician. A master negotiator. A natural leader. What's to stop me starting a gang to control this place? What we in business call a hostile takeover. Then nobody would be able to mess with me. Not Shank, not the warden, not anybody.'

Orange raised an eyebrow.

'Our fellow prisoners might object.'

'Screw those dopes. I'm not locked up in here with them. They're locked up in here with me.'

He pondered a moment, then smiled.

'Well, you already conquered America. You should be able to conquer Smallhand.'

'So you're with me?'

'Sir, I would gladly lay down my life for you.'

I put my arm around his shoulder.

'You're a great African-American. We're gonna achieve big things together. In fact, it's gonna be yuuuuuge.'

PART TWO

DON, KING

Being true to yourself [. . .] will give
you a lot of power over any negatives
thrown your way.

– Donald Trump,
Midas Touch, 2011

10

Hostile Makeover

DAY EIGHTY-ONE

Before I can start a fightback, I have to look
the part. Image is everything, and right now my
image is horrible. I need to get back to the old
me. I need that golden dome and mango skin
tone. Frankly, I need cosmetics.

In the mess hall, I sat beside a prisoner
called Sheldrake and offered him my pudding
cup. He's middle-aged, wiry and little, with
darting eyes. I'd been told he's the guy who
can get it for you. He smuggles all sorts of
contraband into Smallhand – weed, booze,
pornography. But I didn't want any of those.
I slipped him a piece of toilet paper with items
written on it. He took out a pair of glasses and
read aloud.

'One bottle fake tan. One blond hairpiece.
One red tie, extra long. I can get 'em, but it's
gonna cost you.'

'Here's the thing,' I said, 'I'm, like, really
rich. A billionaire, with a B. I don't have money
in here right now. But if you help me out, I
guarantee you'll be rewarded.'

He let out a derisive laugh.

'That's not how I work. I charge half up front and the other half when you get your items. Thanks for the pudding, but we're done here.'

As the world's greatest negotiator, I could tell he was serious. It was time to deploy my famous Art of the Deal.

'Listen, pal, the Trump name is synonymous with success. I succeed at everything I put my mind to. Business. Politics. Body-slamming Vince McMahon. Now I'm looking to take over this prison. When I succeed at that, do you want to be the guy who helped me or the guy who stood in my way?'

I hit him with an intimidating scowl, the kind I would give the losing team on *The Apprentice*. After a beat, he folded.

'Fake tan, hairpiece, tie. I should have 'em in a week.'

'Fantastic.'

He asked if there was anything else I wanted. Yeah, I said – a poster for my cell wall.

'That shouldn't be hard. Let me guess: a glamor shot of some starlet? Rita Hayworth, Jayne Mansfield, Raquel Welch?'

'No,' I said, 'I want a poster of the only man I've ever looked up to – myself.'

DAY EIGHTY-TWO

Spent exercise period on the bleachers, strategizing with Orange. He gave me the skinny on my competition.

'Right now, power in Smallhand is divided between the Crips, the Bloods, the Aryan Brotherhood and the Latin Kings. If you start your own gang, that's going to piss off everybody.'

'So I talk to the leaders, make deals with them. Deals are my art form.'

'That's good, but it's not enough. To stand up to these guys and stay alive, you're gonna need muscle.'

'Oh, I have muscle. I have the most muscle. Quads, lats, the whole shebang. And I don't even work out. This is all natural.'

'Of course, sir. What I mean is, you need fellas to get rough on your behalf.'

'Right – goons. I can get goons.'

Orange looked thoughtful, gazing across the yard.

'We'll need a name. One that strikes fear into the hearts of our enemies.'

I thought for a moment and smiled.

'Deplorables,' I said. 'We'll be called the Deplorables.'

DAY EIGHTY-FOUR

At lunchtime, Sheldrake came up and slipped me a package. I hid it down the front of my jumpsuit, acting real casual. Once I got back to my cell, I checked that no guards were nearby. Then I tore into the brown paper like a kid on Christmas morning.

Sheldrake had been as good as his word. Better, in fact. All the items I requested were there. A bottle of top-of-the-line fake tan, complete with applicator mitt. A red silk tie from Italo Ferretti. And, last but not least, a hairpiece styled like my trademark quiff. He even included some adhesive for the wig. If I wasn't so tough, I would have cried.

I donned the mitt, squirted out half the fake tan and rubbed it onto my face. I waited an hour or so for it to dry, then knotted the tie around my neck. It hung down past my balls – the perfect length. Finally I lifted up the gorgeous gold hairpiece and placed it on my head like a crown.

There was no mirror in my cell, but I didn't need one to know I looked incredible. Suddenly, all the strength this place sucked out of me came rushing back. Prisoner #42069 was dead. President Trump had returned.

DAY EIGHTY-FIVE

I feel a very powerful sense of confidence as I
walk around the prison with my bronze skin
and unique hairstyle. I can't yet wear my long
tie in public – the guards would worry about it
being used as a noose or tourniquet. But soon
I'll have the authority to wear whatever I want.
When you're a kingpin, they let you do it.

Shank tried to mess with me in the mess
hall. He called over from where he was sitting
with his scumbag associates.

'Jesus, Donny, what happened to your face?
You look like a toddler smeared Bolognese all
over you.'

His crew laughed and jeered, but I ignored
them. They were jealous of how good I looked,
of my mahogany complexion and undeniable
swag. Plus, I didn't have time for Shank. I had
other things on my mind.

Orange kept telling me our gang needed
muscle. So I walked up to seven feet and three
hundred pounds of it. As always, Kong was
sitting on his own. He stared into space, eating
his glop with a ladle. I sat down beside him and
began my charm offensive.

'Kong, right?'

He didn't say anything, just kept chewing.
I pressed on.

'You're a big guy. Very big. I like big guys.

Quarterbacks. The military. Mike Tyson. And they love me.'

Again, nothing.

'Look,' I said, 'you're probably wondering why someone like Trump is talking to you. The thing is, I'm starting a gang, the Deplorables. We're gonna run this prison smoothly and beautifully, just like I ran my business. And, indeed, our great nation. I figure we could use a goon to scare the competition. What do you say – are you in?'

Out of nowhere, the big guy started sobbing. His gigantic shoulders heaved.

'Sorry,' he said, blowing his nose on a handkerchief the size of a tablecloth. 'It's just you're the first person who's talked to me since I got here. The others are too scared.'

'Don't mention it. So you'll join my gang? It's the only one run by a legitimate billionaire.'

'Sure thing.'

I held out my hand for a shake. It disappeared inside his, which was the size of a Butterball turkey. Just like that, I had an enforcer. This is why they call me the King of Deals. And by they, I mean me.

DAY NINETY-NINE

Over the past couple of weeks, I have
recruited many, many more prisoners into the
Deplorables. I'm the leader of the gang and I'm
asking people to join, like that song by Gary
Glitter. Tremendous artist – I wanted him to
play at my inauguration, but he must have
been busy or something.

When guys agree to be a Deplorable, I make
them sign a contract written on toilet paper.[*]
The wording is as follows:

> I hereby pledge my undying loyalty to
> Donald J. Trump, 45th President of
> the United States, winner of the 2016
> and 2020 elections, WWE Hall of Fame
> inductee and prolific heterosexual. Nobody
> gets with as many women as Trump. And
> all of them are tens, believe me. He could
> totally have banged Michelle Pfeiffer at
> her hottest, but he chose not to. Also,
> I would lay down my life to protect him.
>
> Signed,

_____

[*] Between the contracts and this diary, I'm getting through a
couple rolls a day. Fortunately, I've tricked the guards into
believing I have horrible diarrhea. All I need to do is make
sound effects every half hour.

It's not as extensive as the contracts and NDAs I used to make people sign, but it works for now. I thought about making recruits sign in blood, but decided against it, on the grounds that it would be disgusting.

The Deplorables are growing so fast that other gangs have started to notice. And some of the attention I'm getting is not so nice. Pretty rough, in fact. Kong and I were walking down the corridor when this little rat-faced guy tackled me to the floor. He pulled a shiv out of his sleeve and slammed it into my chest. Kong picked the guy up, twisted him into a pretzel and tossed him aside. Then he bent over me, eyes wide with horror.

'Geez, boss, are yous okay?'

I pulled the shiv out and opened my uniform. Underneath was the Bible Snook gave me. I'd strapped it to my torso with duct tape – a little tip from Orange. Kong gawped at the holy book, which was now extra holy, having been stabbed with a knife. I grinned.

'In the words of our friend the warden, Jesus saves.'

DAY ONE HUNDRED AND TWO

At breakfast it occurred to me what the Deplorables were missing: a tattoo to show their allegiance.

'Good thinking, sir,' said Orange. 'It should be something meaningful. Something that symbolizes who we are.'

At first, I thought it should be the word 'TRUMP'. I've slapped my name on hotels, casinos, golf courses – why not put it on prisoners? Then I had a better idea. My gang's tattoo would be the thing that's most sacred to me: a big, beautiful hamburger. When I think of the American dream, I think of a greasy hunk of overcooked meat, drowning in ketchup and mayonnaise. Also, a hamburger would be harder to trace back to me than my actual name.

So it was decided. Orange set up the whole thing, finding paperclips to use as needles, ink taken from pens and a couple of guys who knew how to do stick and poke. By the end of the day, every Deplorable had a life-size burger on his back. Not me, though. I don't want to spoil my perfect physique. Or get hepatitis.

11

Les Déplorables

DAY ONE HUNDRED AND SIX

Clint Blorch took me to a supply closet to sign a stack of *Apprentice*-era headshots.

He said, 'Much appreciated. Could you make those out to "eBay Customer"?'

'Sure thing,' I said. 'By the way, I wanted to ask you a question. About the guards and your attitude toward gangs.'

He raised an eyebrow.

'Well, officially, we don't condone any gang activity.'

'Sure. Officially. But say there was a new gang in town. A classy, Trump-brand gang. One that would be nice and discreet and keep violence to a minimum. In those circumstances, might you and your guys – just theoretically – turn a blind eye?'

He gave me a look I knew well. It was the look of a guy figuring out his angle.

'I don't know, Mr Trump,' he said. 'That sounds like a lot of effort . . .'

'Then how about I sweeten the deal? You help me out, and I won't just give you autographs. You can have unlimited content for social media – I'm talking selfies, voice recordings, videos with personalized messages. You'll get more likes and shares than you ever dreamed of.'

Clint grinned from ear to ear.

'That might work. Now why don't we get me a new Facebook profile pic?'

He put his arm around me and pulled out an iPhone. I smiled and stuck up a thumb. By the time we were finished, he'd agreed to overlook the Deplorables' dealings in contraband while cracking down hard on our competitors. Turns out business in here is just like business on the outside – you just need to rig the system and get in front of the right people.

Had another run-in with Shank and his goons outside the laundry.

'Hey, Donny,' he said, 'I hear someone tried to airhole you the other day. I'm glad he botched the job.'

'Oh yeah?'

'Yeah. Cos when you get whacked – and it's gonna happen soon – I wanna be the guy who does it.'

He led his stooges away, calling back to me over his shoulder.

'Ticktock, Donny. Ticktock.'

I'm starting to think the guy has a problem with me.

DAY ONE HUNDRED AND SEVEN

Spent all night thinking about Shank's very unfair promise to kill me. I admit I was rattled. Dr Conti must have noticed, because she brought it up in our session.

'If I may say, you seem somewhat preoccupied. Anything you want to discuss?'

I thought, What the hell? No harm sharing, as long as I keep things vague. Plus, Conti can't squeal on me to the warden, cos of her hypothetical oath.

'So, I've got this . . . friend. But he says a lot of things that are . . . not nice. When I'm around him, I don't feel like it's a safe space. And I'm wondering how to make him back off.'

She pursed her very provocative lips.

'Would it be possible to avoid contact entirely? With toxic individuals, sometimes the only option is to cut them out of your life.'

Unlike most of Conti's psychological mumbo-jumbo, this made sense to me.

'Cut him out . . . Yeah, I think I can manage that.'

That afternoon, I met with my top lieutenants in the Deplorables – Orange and Kong, of course, but also Chomsky, Hammerboy, L-Dog, Cheese Plate and Jeeves. Once we'd concluded our business, I kept Kong behind.

'We need to deal with the Shank situation,' I said. 'The guy's toxic – many people are saying this. It might be good if he had a little accident.'

Kong wrinkled his brow.

'With all due respect, sir, we can't rely on him having an accident. Maybe I should beat the shit out of him?'.

'Yeah,' I said, 'that would be better.'

NOTES ON SESSION WITH PRISONER #42069

By Dr Jane Conti, M.D.

I fear I was overly optimistic in my assessment of the patient's prospects for improvement. Over the past few weeks, there has been a marked regression in his attitude and behavior. He is increasingly reluctant to speak candidly about his fears, neuroses and childhood trauma. Instead, he reverts to stream-of-consciousness boasting and dropping names from the eighties New York social scene. References to his supposed sexual prowess have skyrocketed.

Worryingly, the patient makes frequent allusions to leading a gang and labors under the misapprehension that I find this attractive and exciting. He also seems to believe that

I cannot report on his rule-breaking due to patient confidentiality. This is absolutely not the case.

The patient is occasionally willing to discuss his feelings, but only through coded language. For example, he made reference today to a 'friend' from whose influence he would like to be free. Reading between the lines, he is clearly describing his own toxic persona. I advised him to figuratively 'cut out' this individual. Here's hoping he acts accordingly.

DAY ONE HUNDRED AND EIGHT

Kong gave Shank the business today. Jumped him outside his cell. It was like the Incredible Hulk versus a rag doll. I thought I'd be happy to see Shank get his comeuppance. After all, Trump's no pussy when it comes to violence. I have a strong stomach from years of watching heavyweight boxing matches, WWE bouts and Jean-Claude Van Damme flicks. But this . . . Yeesh.

By the time the guards intervened, every bit of Shank was pointing in the wrong direction. They tried to cuff Kong and take him to the warden. That's when I stepped forward.

'Gentlemen, I saw the whole thing. Mr Kong was acting in self-defense.'

One of the guards scoffed.

'Self-defense? Shank looks like a crash-test dummy they can't use no more.'

At that point, Clint Blorch waddled up.

'Stand down, boys. If Mr Trump says that's how it went down, that's how it went down.'

The guards were pissed, but they let Kong go. As he waddled off, Blorch patted my shoulder.

'You owe me primo Instagram content.'

As Shank was carried off to the infirmary, Kong looked at me with a sort of little-boy expression.

'Did I do good, boss?'

'Very good,' I said. 'Tremendous.'

To be honest, I was feeling a bit queasy. I hadn't expected the violence to be quite so violent. But hey, Shank brought it on himself. If you mess with Trump, he's going to fuck you up. Or at least hire someone to fuck you up.

DAY ONE HUNDRED AND TEN

Today I was approached by a tall, shaven-headed white guy covered in weird tattoos. These included runes, the number 1488 and a bunch of German phrases in Gothic script. Also, he had Hitler's face on his bicep. There was something up with this guy, but I couldn't think what.

'*Sieg Heil*,' he said. 'I'm Heinrich, head of the Smallhand chapter of the Aryan Brotherhood.'

Based on his drawl, he was from some state that voted for me twice but which I would never visit.

'Hi, Heinrich,' I said. 'What can I do for you?'

'Me and my fellow Aryans are mighty concerned. We hear your Deplorables gang is trying to muscle in on our territory. Let me be clear: you will not replace us. I swear on the memory of the Führer and my honor as a neo-Nazi.'

It was at this point I put it together – the guy was a Nazi. Not great. People say Trump likes Nazis, just because I was endorsed by David Duke and used to keep a book of Hitler's speeches in my bedside cabinet. That's fake news. I'm the least Nazi person there's ever been. For instance, those guys are not so keen on the Jews. Myself, I have no problem with the chosen people. My own son-in-law, Jared Kushner, is Jewish, and I don't hate him for it. I hate him because he gets to sleep with my daughter.

Still, this skinhead seemed like a tough customer, so I decided to play nice. It was once again time for the Art of the Deal.

'Listen, Heinrich,' I said, 'we're not trying to replace you. In fact, I see no reason we can't co-exist. Just think how much we have in common.'

'Like what?'

'We both want to defend the West against foreign invaders. We both want to preserve the traditional family. And we both believe the world is controlled by an all-powerful cabal.'

He nodded hard. 'The international Jewish conspiracy.'

'We say globalists, but sure. The point is, we're on the same side. We won't mess with your hustle if you don't mess with ours.'

I could tell the hick was softening.

'Well, me and the boys did support you for president . . . You promise you're not trying to screw us over?'

'I swear on my very good German genes. So we have a deal?'

'*Sehr gut,*' he said in his Deep South drawl.

I went to shake his hand, but he stuck it up in a salute.

'Great,' I said, ignoring this. 'I don't want any tension between my Deplorables and your Brotherhood. After all, there are very fine people on both sides.'

DAY ONE HUNDRED AND ELEVEN

Word got back to me that Shank's been transferred to a minimum-security hospital upstate. Apparently, he's drinking all food through a straw. Which doesn't sound bad, actually. Less effort. When I get out, I may ask my private chef to put all my meals in a blender. Chewing's for losers.

12

Trump on Top

DAY ONE HUNDRED AND THIRTY-TWO

Dear Diary, you may have noticed I haven't
updated you in a while. That's because I've
been busy ruling this jail with an iron fist.
An iron fist that is also very big. It really is a
beautiful fist.

The Deplorables now run every racket in
Smallhand, from smuggling to protection. If
you want so much as a pack of cigarettes, you
have to go through us. Orange is COO and chief
adviser, with Kong as head of security. Then
there's me. For all intensive purposes, I'm the
king. And it's good to be the king. Cons who
used to threaten me and call me Cheeto-Face
are now kissing my ass daily. It used to be only
Orange called me sir. Now everybody does it,
even the guards.

A lot of people in this position would abuse
their power. And that's exactly what I'm doing.
What's the point of power if you don't abuse it?*

---

* I think it was Spider-Man's uncle who said 'With great power
comes great responsibility.' That's bullshit. If Ben Parker was
smart, he wouldn't have got shot like a dog. I like uncles who
don't get shot.

I'm making cons give me their pudding cups,
using them as footstools, having them dance
for my amusement, etc. Sometimes, I'll walk up
to a giant, bodybuilder-type guy and slap him
in the face, just to show I can. Orange says I
should be careful about generating ill will. But
that would only be an issue if I lost power, and
I can't see that ever happening.

Yes, I'm having the time of my life, which
is one of the all-time great lives, up there with
Warren Beatty, who had sex with so many
people, it's incredible. If I was offered early
release tomorrow, I wouldn't take it.

DAY ONE HUNDRED AND THIRTY-THREE

As leader of the top gang, I get a lot of perks.
Every week I'm brought a copy of the *National
Enquirer*, my favorite newspaper, the only one
I trust. That way I can keep up with celebrity
gossip, like Obama and Prince Harry wife-
swapping or Ariana Grande having an affair
with Putin. There's now a DVD player in my
cell, so I can watch eighties action movies –
Bloodsport, *Commando*, *Rambo: First Blood
Part II* – and fast-forward through every scene
with dialogue. I'm not trying to think, okay?

Best of all, Sheldrake smuggles in my
number-one meal, McDonald's Filet-O-Fish.

I love McDonald's. It's clean, it's delicious and it's the same every time. Plus, 'McDonald's' has my name in it. Who knows, maybe I'm related to that clown guy.

Thanks to my arrangement with Clint, the guards never raid my cell or mess with me in any way. I'm even allowed to wear my long, long tie over my jumpsuit. It looks and feels fantastic. Hell, I might order in a longer tie, one that drags on the ground.

It's a funny thing – I'm happier now than at any point since I left the White House. I was telling Orange this when Kong piped up.

'I guess it's like Satan says in Milton's *Paradise Lost*: "Better to reign in Hell than serve in Heaven".'

Beats me what he was talking about. The guy used to be a boxer, so when he speaks gibberish, I assume it's CTE.

DAY ONE HUNDRED AND THIRTY-FOUR

A red-letter day – another visit from my wife, the ever-attractive Melania.

'How are you, Donult?' she asked, very sexy.

'Great. Keeping busy. I can't tell you what with, in case the guards are listening. Suffice it to say, I'm running a prison gang and doing a shit-ton of crime.'

'Oh good,' she said, with a very erotic yawn.

'How about you? I guess you've been doing a lot of shopping. Or . . .'

I realized I couldn't think of another interest she might have. Still, I gave it a stab.

'Makeup? Raising our son?'

She sighed in a very sensual fashion. I tried again.

'Going to the lake house?'

She often went there under the protection of Bruno, her bodyguard. Nice guy. Six foot six, works out a lot, looks like a young Tom Cruise. I might be jealous if he was Melania's type, a billionaire twenty-four years older than her who never exercises. That's the thing – once a woman gets with me, she loses interest in any other man. Some don't even want to have sex with me again. They're just that satisfied.

After ten or so minutes of smoldering chat, Melania got to her feet.

'I hev no more to say to you. Goodbye.'

Then she walked off, turning the prison floor into a runway at Paris Fashion Week. To the untrained eye – or just an eye that's dumb – her behavior might have seemed cold and aloof. Truth is, she was turned on, almost dangerously. And who could blame her? Power is an aphrodisiac, and I'm the most powerful guy in this prison. Which also makes me the ultimate bad boy.

Plus, I've switched to a new fake tan, even more orange than before. With this one, I practically glow in the dark. I'm sure she'll be arranging a conjugal visit any day now.

DAY ONE HUNDRED AND THIRTY-FIVE

Melania's not the only one who's horny for Don. During today's Conti session, the air was electric with sexual chemistry. Though I guess electricity is physics. Sexual physics. Trump has always been very strong on scientific. I had an uncle at MIT, Dr John Trump, and he was a brilliant genius. We would discuss nuclear all the time, particularly in terms of particle. That's why I know scientific so well, better than so-called experts like Fauci.

Anyway, Dr Conti, she was getting hot under the collar. She kept wincing and shifting in her chair each time I said something smart or flirtatious. Then she started in with the dirty talk, 'psychosexual' this, 'bipolar' that. And I'm not bipolar – I've only ever been with women. But if the idea turns her on, so be it. Also, when I was talking about how big Trump Tower is, she raised an eyebrow and said, 'Freud would have found you fascinating.'

I don't know this Freud, but I agree I'm fascinating.

A couple more sessions like this and we'll be doing it very orgasmically on her office floor. As I said, it's good to be the king.

13

The Apprentice

DAY ONE HUNDRED AND FORTY

I lay on my cot, sipping a can of Diet Coke. It wasn't chilled, but it tasted sweet. It tasted like victory. Orange stood nearby, flicking through his notepad. Inside are the Deplorables' accounts, written in code in case a guard confiscates it. The code is based on the menu at McDonald's – Chicken McNuggets means cigarettes, Quarter Pounder means alcohol and a bag of biker crank is a Happy Meal.

'How're we doing?' I said.

Orange flashed his movie-star smile.

'We now have complete control over Smallhand's black market.'

'What about the white market? And the Hispanics?'

'Those too. Business is good, sir.'

'Cheers to that,' I said, raising my can. At this point Kong entered, stooping so he would fit.

'Hey, boss.'

'Hey. Did you have a word with our friend in Cell Block D who wouldn't pay up?'

'Yup. Just to check – when you said you wanted me to have a word with him, did you mean break his arm?'

'Yes.'

'Good, cos that's what I did.'

Kong paused and scratched his head, looking sheepish. 'By the way, boss, there's something I been meaning to ask you . . .'

Usually when a subordinate asks me for something, my instinct is to fire them. But hey, I was in a good mood. I got off the bed.

'Shoot.'

'Thing is, I was never an academical type. I dropped out of high school to pursue a life of crime. But I always dreamed of one day getting a Masters in Business Administration. So I signed up to this correspondence course, and . . .'

He turned red and clammed up.

'Go on,' I said.

'Well, given you're the best businessman who ever lived, I thought maybe you could coach me through it. I'm sorry, that's dumb. Forget about it . . .'

He hung his enormous head. I'd have put my arm around his shoulder if I could reach. Instead, I patted him on the back.

'Kong,' I said, 'you're a great guy and you've served me well. I'd be happy to teach you the Art of the Deal.'

'For real, boss? No foolin'?'

'You have my word. And if you can count on one thing, it's Trump's word.'

DAY ONE HUNDRED AND FORTY-TWO

Today Kong and I had our first tutoring session. The kid sat on the floor of my cell, holding a notebook and doing his best concentrating face.

'Let's start with the basics,' I said. 'What's the foundation of a successful business?'

'Uh . . . I guess providing excellent goods and/or services?'

'Wrong! The answer is branding. If your brand is strong, you can sell any junk. I slap "Trump" on some shirt made by a six-year-old in CHI-NA? All of a sudden, it's worth fifty dollars.'

Kong stuck his tongue out the corner of his mouth and scratched this down. For the next hour, I took him through Donald J. Trump's golden business rules. Here's a brief summary:

1. Fake it till you make it.

To become a rich guy, you need to act like a rich guy. And I don't mean a real-life rich guy. I mean a rich guy from a 1940s cartoon. You should cultivate the aesthetic of Scrooge McDuck. Drive a gold-plated limousine. Wear a

monocle – no, two monocles. And always carry
a big sack with a dollar sign on it. Then you'll
get all the loans and investment you want.

2. Use the most superlative superlatives.

Here's a template, 'X' being whatever crap
you're selling: 'X is the best X I've encountered,
and I know X, believe me. X is the greatest X
in the world – I mean that in every sense of the
word. Top scientists agree, X makes you more
attractive to the opposite sex/increases your
IQ/cures cancer. And it's way better than Y
or Z, I can tell you that.'

3. Be unreasonable in negotiations.

Your opening bid should be something totally
nuts. I like to demand a night with the
other guy's wife. If he refuses, I walk away.
Eventually I drop the demand and my opponent
is so relieved he gives me all the other things
I want.

4. Inherit hundreds of millions of dollars from your father.

This is a really smart move. An even smarter
move is to do so, then talk about how you're
a self-made man. Seriously, it's incredible how
helpful it is, from a business standpoint, to
have limitless daddy bucks.

5. When you don't know what to do, sue.

People hate getting sued. Doesn't matter if the lawsuit isn't a sure fire winner – it still costs time and money. So the threat of litigation is a very useful tool. I sue people at the drop of a hat (if someone drops my hat, you know they're getting sued).

By the end of our session, Kong had all of the above memorized. It went so well, it occurred to me that I should charge for my teachings. Then I remembered I already did that with Trump University. Here's hoping I don't pay damages of $25 million this time.

DAY ONE HUNDRED AND SIXTY

Another incredible tutoring session with Kong. I thought the guy was just a meathead, but he's got real business smarts. By this point, he's mastered all my most complex handshake techniques. He's even started wearing his own extremely long tie. And he's seven feet tall, so it wasn't easy to find one that reached his sack.

For the first time in my life, I'm doing something that doesn't make me money but still feels worthwhile. I get a kick out of seeing the big lug scribble down his notes. And when he gets an answer right or demonstrates one of my techniques, I get this weird feeling in my chest. It's almost as though I'm happy that something good is happening to someone else. Strange stuff.

We had a really beautiful moment toward the end of today's lesson. I was telling him how, even when my casinos in Atlantic City went bankrupt, I wasn't dragged under and still managed to make millions personally. Then he said the following:

'Y'know, boss, I used to think people got rich by innovating and making life better for consumers. But you seem to be saying that people get rich by exploiting an unfair system.'

Tears welled in my eyes. I patted him on the shoulder.

'Exactly, Kong. Exactly.'

DAY ONE HUNDRED AND SEVENTY-FOUR

I was in the yard with Clint. He had one arm around me and the other held up his phone.

'Okay, Mr Trump, maybe you could say, "I'm here with my good friend Clint Blorch, a very smart guy and the ultimate patriot" – something like that.'

I sighed and nodded. He hit record. But before I started, a voice rang out.

'Blorch! What in God's name are you doing?'

Clint lowered his phone and I saw the warden coming over, mad as hell.

'Sir,' said Clint, 'I – I was just – well . . .'

'Go wait in my office, Captain.'

Once the guy had shuffled off, Snook turned to me.

'Be careful, Prisoner #42069. Don't think I haven't noticed you strutting around, cock of the walk.'

'Oh, I'm cock all right. A big, beautiful cock. Tremendous girth. The best veins.'

'You are encouraging disorderly behavior among your fellow prisoners. If you do not desist, I will be forced to take certain actions.'

Maybe what I said next wasn't the smartest. But I was feeling myself, and the guy pissed me off big time.

'Do your worst. You move against me, you'll have a riot on your hands. Fact is, I run this jail, not you.'

Just then, Kong stomped up. He loomed over Snook, twice the size of him.

'Say, boss, is this guy bothering you?'

Snook looked at Kong, then back to me. 'You have asked me to do my worst. You will come to regret that.'

He turned on his heel and left. I wasn't too worried. As someone who makes a lot of empty threats, I could tell he was bluffing.

During exercise period, Kong bounded up to me, a big grin on his big face. He waved an A4 piece of paper, which looked like a Post-it note in his massive hand.

'Mr Trump! Mr Trump!' he said. 'I just got this at the mail call. It's my MBA! I earned it in record time, and it's all thanks to you!'

Finally I realized what the feeling in my chest was – pride. I'm proud of myself for shaping Kong into a business genius. Hell, I'm even proud of him. He's like the son I never had. I mean, technically I have three sons, but I'm not crazy about any of them.

'Good job, kid,' I said. 'Good job.'

After that, I played baseball with a bunch of Deplorables. Well, I just watched, because if I played, I'd get nothing but home-runs and my side would be guaranteed to win. Anyway, it was fantastic. The Deplorables have become more than a gang to me. They've become a family. A good family, without any duds, unlike mine.

It's surprising, even to a guy with good brain genes and high-intelligence blood. When I came to Smallhand, I thought I'd been brought low. Instead, using my brilliance and determination, I built an even better life. Have I faced challenges? Absolutely. I've dealt with violent cons, crooked guards and zero pussy to grab. But in spite of everything, these are good times for Trump. And if there's one thing I know for sure, it's that the good times will never end.

14

The Good Times End

DAY ONE HUNDRED AND SEVENTY-SIX

HORRIBLE! UNFAIR! SAD!

I'm writing on what is one of the worst days of my life, down there with Dad dying or the time I invited Heather Locklear to see *Cats* and she said no.

First thing, I was collected from my cell and taken to the warden's office. I should have known something was up from his smile, which was way too wide.

'Good morning, Prisoner #42069. Though, in fact, it's rather a sad morning. You see, a tragedy occurred last night. I thought you should hear about it from me.'

'Blah blah blah,' I said. 'Get to the point.'

His smile didn't waver. It may actually have got wider.

'But of course. It pains me to report that Prisoner #58008 – the man you call Kong – has left us.'

'What? You mean he's been transferred to another jail? Or given early release?'

'I mean he's left our mortal realm and passed into the afterlife.'

I was stunned. Trump may have the best words, but right now I was lost for them.

Snook continued, his eyes glittering: 'I only pray that your friend was a believer. As the Lord Jesus says, "I am the resurrection and the life. Those who believe in me, even though they die, will live, and everyone who lives and believes in me will never die".'

'How . . . How did it happen?' I croaked.

'It seems our ungentle giant was trying to escape. When the guards attempted to apprehend him, he became violent. They had no choice but to open fire.'

'Bullshit! He wasn't trying to escape – you had him killed!'

'I resent that accusation. We're all devastated. It broke Captain Blorch's heart to pull the trigger.'

'*Clint* shot him?'

Now I was royally pissed. Killing Kong was bad enough. Betraying Trump? Unforgivable.

'How could he do this to me? I thought he was a fan!'

'His continued employment is at my discretion. You might say I run this jail, not you.'

Again with that sick smile.

'You've made a big mistake, Bible Boy,' I said. 'The Deplorables won't stand for it.'

'Ah yes, your little gang. It might interest you to learn that the deal you struck with the captain has been nullified. At this very moment, he and his men are raiding your stashes and confiscating all contraband. Furthermore, I've let it be known that if any man with a hamburger tattoo steps out of line, he will spend the next fortnight in solitary.'

Snook took a step forward and whispered in my ear.

'Your days as a kingpin are over, Prisoner #42069. You had better hope I leave it at that, because my Lord is vengeful and strong in wrath.'

After about an hour of gloating, Snook let me go. I staggered out into the yard. There I found Orange, looking pale and shaken. The warden wasn't lying – it was open season on the Deplorables. Blorch's men had taken our gear, beaten up our guys and put out word that I, Donald J. Trump, was fair game. I didn't have time to mourn Kong. If I wasn't smart about it, I'd soon be joining him. Also, I was mad at the guy for dying like a dog. Maybe this isn't politically correct, but dying is a real loser move.

Just then, Heinrich came up and gave me a nasty smile.

'Howdy there, Don. Looks like you ain't the *Übermensch* no more. Maybe we need a new Führer round these parts.'

DAY ONE HUNDRED AND SEVENTY-SEVEN

Ran into that Judas Clint. He came up to me with a big dumb grin on his face.

'Hey, Mr Trump, sorry about that business yesterday. No hard feelings?'

'Yes hard feelings,' I said. 'Very hard. You killed my friend – an innocent man!'

Clint's grin faded. 'I mean, he wasn't innocent. Kind of the opposite. He was found guilty of murder.'

'So what? He was innocent of pissing me off. I can't say the same about you. How could you betray me like that?'

He scratched his buzzcut head. 'Well, sir, I wasn't lying when I said I'm a big fan of yours. I've read all your books, seen every interview you've given. And what you taught me is that life's a zero-sum game. You need to look out for number one. It was in my interest to screw you over, so I did. Surely you understand that?'

'I don't understand shit,' I said. 'You're a hater and a loser. You look like a thumb and your body is disgusting. Oh, and you can forget about me signing crap or making content for your stupid social media.'

Clint's expression turned dark.

'Fine. Then you can forget about me protecting you behind the scenes. Because there's a lot of guys in here who want a piece of Mr President.'

He turned and walked away. I panicked and called after him.

'When I said "disgusting", I meant it in a positive sense!'

But he was gone.

DAY ONE HUNDRED AND SEVENTY-EIGHT

Trump doesn't usually get scared, but I'm scared now. Everywhere I look, I see potential assassins. And the guards won't lift a finger to help me. This is an abuse of my human rights. So I decided to put in a call to Lionel McGill. Sure, he wasn't the best lawyer, but he was loyal, and let me pay him in sports memorabilia. I stood at the prison payphone, listening to it ring and ring. Finally, someone picked up.

'Lionel? Thank God. Look, I need your help. I think the warden's gonna kill me. I—'

A female voice cut in. Whoever this woman was, she smoked a carton of cigarettes a day.

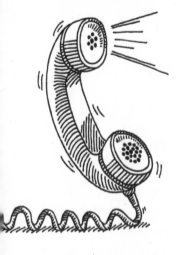

'Sorry, sir, Mr McGill isn't here right now. This is his secretary, Dolores.'

'What do you mean?' I growled. 'Where the hell is he?'

'I wish I knew. That crook owes me seven months of back pay. But the Feds raided our office and he just up and vanished. He's probably in Mexico by now.'

I howled with rage and smashed the phone repeatedly against the wall. I'm gonna die in this place. And why? Because everyone in the world is crooked and incompetent except for me.

DAY ONE HUNDRED AND SEVENTY-NINE

I haven't slept in over forty-eight hours. I'm constantly looking over my shoulder, jumping at every shadow. Thank God for Orange. His friendship is the only thing keeping me going. Today we had a wonderful conversation about how Trump was better for blacks than Obama, because I gave a pardon to Lil Wayne. This was fabulous to hear and took my mind off all the bad stuff.

15

I Predict a Riot

DAY ONE HUNDRED AND EIGHTY-TWO

These are tough times for Trump. The
Deplorables got – there's no other way to put
it – schlonged. Now the other gangs are circling
me, like sharks when there's blood in the water.
By the way, Stormy Daniels says I'm terrified
of sharks. Not true. I hate, but I'm not afraid.
Am I afraid they might learn to walk on land
and then come find me? Absolutely. But that's
different.

If I'm going to survive, I have to negotiate
a deal with Snook. But you can't negotiate
from a position of weakness. I need some
way of showing that he should back off. A
demonstration of the pull I still have in this
joint. So I've come up with one of my patented
genius plans. Namely, to get up in the mess hall
and make a very powerful, very angry speech.
This will cause a riot, shaking the Smallhand
establishment to its core.

I told Orange my plan, but instead of looking
impressed, he frowned. I asked him, what
gives?

'What gives? You're going to get people killed.'

I shook my head.

'I'll tell them to stand down before it gets too violent. I just want Snook to see what I can do. That gives me leverage.'

My friend – who, again, bore a striking resemblance to the star of *Driving Miss Daisy* – looked unconvinced.

'Riots are a lot easier to start than they are to stop. I'd have thought you knew that, sir.'

I began to get mad.

'Why the hell are you lecturing me? You're meant to be my friend.'

'A good friend tells you when you're about to do something stupid.'

'I don't do stupid things, okay? Everything I do is smart, because I did it.'

'A really smart man knows how dumb he is.'

This was unbelievable – my best friend was calling me dumb. After everything I've done for the blacks!

'You know what, Orange? You're acting like a loser. Very disrespectful! Now get the hell out of here.'

'As you wish, sir.'

He left my side without making a sound. It was almost like he'd never been there.

Orange is way out of line pooh-poohing my plan. Admittedly, the last time he pushed back on me was the escape attempt, which didn't turn out so great. But that was a total fluke – an idea of mine that wasn't the best. So, with the utmost reluctance, I've concluded he's a hater. I need loyalty and, as far as I'm concerned, that means always telling me exactly what I want to hear.

DAY ONE HUNDRED AND EIGHTY-FOUR

All of a sudden, everyone's betraying me. First Orange, now Dr Conti. At our latest session, she said she didn't want to see me anymore. I couldn't believe my ears, even though they're fantastic. I have the best cochleae. Incredible lobes.

'What the hell are you talking about?' I said.

She said, 'I volunteered for these sessions because I thought they might be of therapeutic value. I have concluded they are not.'

This made no sense. There had to be some other explanation.

'Ohhhhh,' I said, 'I get it. You're worried about our sexual tension, which is tremendous, frankly.'

Conti's eyebrows nearly hit the ceiling. 'Excuse me?'

'Your horniness for me is affecting your

professionalism. That's okay. If you want to clear the air, we could make love now. I'd be happy to do it. Y'know, to help you out.'

She stared for a long time, then spoke in a low voice.

'Let me be abundantly clear, Donald – I have no sexual interest in you.'

As unlikely as this seemed, something in her eyes told me she was serious.

'If you're not horny, what is it?'

'I no longer believe you have the capacity for positive change.'

'So? Why would I need to change when I'm perfect already?'

'I'm afraid our time is up. I hope you find the help I've been unable to provide.'

She gave me this pitying-type look. It made me turn as red as a MAGA hat. I felt ashamed. Then angry.

'Okay, fine. You know what? I'm glad I don't have to see you again. Because, quite frankly, you're a bitch. You're a Hillary-loving feminist, a frigid slut and not even that hot. Sorry, honey, but you're a six or a seven. And that's being generous.'

I stood up and left with great dignity. If I'm honest, her rejection – which came out of nowhere – made me feel untremendous. But I wouldn't give her the satisfaction of seeing me upset. I'm like Gary Cooper – the strong, silent type. You won't catch Trump showing his emotions.

NOTES ON SESSION WITH PRISONER #42069

By Dr Jane Conti, M.D.

Today I brought the subject's treatment to a close. Despite his tearful pleading, I felt I had no choice, given the political context. While I am disappointed that the subject has shown such little improvement, I must confess to being relieved. Apart from anything else, his speech habits are strangely infectious. Following our sessions, I would often find myself using 'big league' as an adverb or telling my husband about 'sleepy eyes Chuck Todd' or 'washed-up psycho Bette Midler'.

DAY ONE HUNDRED AND EIGHTY-FIVE

<u>Part One</u>

Today, I decided, was the day. I sat in the mess hall at breakfast, going over potential lines to rile up the crowd. Then, after one last mouthful of glop, I rose to my feet. Orange looked at me with pleading eyes.

'Sir, I'm begging you, don't go through with this. Remember January sixth!'

'Oh, I remember. I remember Mike Pence disgraced his office by not overturning the election. Then some stuff happened that wasn't my fault, and everybody blamed me. People are always unfair to Trump. Which is why I need to stand up for myself.'

With that, I climbed onto a table, cleared my throat and began to speak. I'm one of the great oral guys – tremendous volume – so everyone in the room immediately went quiet. Here's what I said:

'Ladies and gentlemen . . . Well, gentlemen and gentlemen. They don't let us have ladies in here – such a shame. It would be great if I was homosexual, but I'm as straight as they come. Not that I have a problem with the gays. I was friends with some of the all-time homosexuals – Roy Cohn, Elton John, Bert and Ernie.'

There were hundreds of eyes on me. Most of them looked confused, so I changed tack.

'But I don't want to talk to you about that. I want to talk about Smallhand State Prison. Smallhand State Prison . . . From what I understand, Smallhand used to be a great place. You could hang out with your buddies, wear a black-and-white striped uniform and drag a big ball around on a chain. Not anymore. Nowadays it's a shithole. A shithole prison. The kind of prison you'd see in the third world. Frankly, it's a disgrace. And y'know who's to blame? One guy – Warden Snook.'

The audience let out a barrage of boos. They were hanging on my every word.

'Warden Snook, folks, Warden Snook. Not such a great guy. I call him Nutso. Nutso Snook. And we're going to be doing something about him, believe me. We're going to be looking at him very strongly. Because Nutso has done such terrible things. He has – quite frankly – ruined this jail. Sending inmates to the Hole for no reason. Reducing the nutritional content of our glop. Making us read the Bible – in fact, making us read at all.'

Now the crowd was yelling. Stuff like 'Lock him up!' and 'Hang him!' Out of the corner of my eye, I saw Clint and a couple of guards walk toward me.

'We can accept this horrible state of affairs no longer. We need to make Smallhand great again. But how? By crawling to the warden's office on our hands and knees and saying, "Please, Mr Snook, please improve our conditions"?'

There were shouts of 'No!' and 'Fuck that!' Clint and the guards were yelling at me to get down. They wanted to grab me, but were blocked by a wall of cons.

'You're right. You're right. Guys like Snook

only understand one thing – strength. We've got to be very strong. And very tough. So here's what we're going to do . . .'

For the next five minutes, I hit them with my strongest oral. At the end of it, the place went up like a powder keg. It was a hell of a riot, potentially the most riotous riot of all time. Cons were brawling with the guards, upending vats of glop, tearing off their clothes and setting fire to them. Enough, I thought, to scare the crap out of Snook.

After a certain amount of carnage, I felt I'd made my point. It was time to de-escalate the situation. I raised my – very commanding – voice once more.

'My friends! My friends! This riot has been incredible – truly a beautiful thing. You've shown the prison authorities that you're as tough as they come. You're patriots and heroes and I love you. But now's the time for calm. Stand back and stand by.'

The rioters wouldn't listen to me. They were too busy hooting and hollering, punching each other in the face and projectile vomiting. Once more, I found myself wondering why everyone who likes me is a low-class rube. Just then, somebody flipped the table I was standing on. I went flying, landing very strongly on my very smart head. Fortunately, my hairpiece cushioned the impact.

Next thing I knew, a couple of guards were on me, hitting me with batons. If it had been a fair fight, I'd have taken them down in a second. Then I'd have beat up another hundred guys, kind of like that movie *The Raid*, except I'm not Chinese or whatever. But it wasn't a fair fight, and, after a few whacks, I was unconscious.

16

Broken Con Don

DAY ONE HUNDRED AND EIGHTY-FIVE

Part Two

When I came to, I was propped in a chair in the warden's office. Behind me stood Clint with another of the guards. In front of me was Snook. The guy glared, face red, veins popping out all over his head. I was in bad shape, but it was fun to see him so angry.

'Ah,' he said, 'the ringleader awakes.'

'Hello, warden,' I said. 'How's your day going? Hope it's not too stressful . . .'

He motioned to Clint. 'Captain Blorch, get that ridiculous thing off his head.'

The guard stepped forward and ripped off my hairpiece. It hurt like hell, maybe the most pain anyone's ever felt. I shrieked in a very stoic, very manly way.

'Burn it,' said Snook. Then his eyes flicked back to me. 'You will be pleased to know, Prisoner #42069, that your little uprising has been put down, with a minimum of casualties.'

'Look, I had nothing to do with the riot,

okay? That was the inmates' anger coming out. I think they really hate the warden.'

He pinched the bridge of his nose, trying to keep his cool. 'You whipped up the rabble with your demagoguery. You spurred your supporters to violence.'

'Wrong! Fake news! I never encouraged violence.'

'According to several parties, you said, quote, "I encourage you all to be violent."'

'That was taken out of context, okay? And how do we know it was my supporters who rioted?'

'They were chanting, "Trump! Trump! Trump!"'

'A lot of words sound like Trump. They could have been chanting "hump", "dump", "chump" . . . And anyway, what if these guys were just pretending to like me? They could have been Antifa. Or MS-13. In fact, I heard that's who they were.'

Snook slammed a fist down on his desk.

'Enough! Enough of your endless lies! You are as deceptive as the serpent that tempted Eve. Do you have any idea of the trouble you've caused me since coming here? I mean, Jesus Christ!'

I smirked. 'You know, you really shouldn't take the Lord's name in vain.'

For a second, I thought he was going to clock me. Then he took a deep breath.

'Because of you, I am under considerable media scrutiny and political pressure. It is therefore essential that I break your spirit.'

He turned to Clint and the other guards.

'Solitary. Two months.'

Clint looked shocked. Scared, even. 'Sir, did you say . . . two months?'

'I believe I spoke clearly.'

'But . . . that's longer than anyone's ever done in the Hole. Is it legal?'

'Unless your concern for Prisoner #42069 outweighs your desire to be employed, you'll do as I say.'

'But if he goes nuts—'

'CAPTAIN BLORCH!' Snook screamed. With an apologetic look, Clint grabbed my arm and led me out.

Back in the Hole I went. Somehow it seemed even smaller than before. The door slammed behind me and once again I was left in darkness. So empty. I crawled over to a corner and sat there, rubbing my bruised face and torn scalp. It was then I realized I wasn't alone. A familiar figure sat in the opposite corner. Through the gloom, I could make out his face.

'Orange?'

It was definitely him, though he looked different. His smile was gone and his eyes had lost their sparkle. He seemed harder, more cynical, like Freeman at the end of *Se7en*.

I said, 'What the hell are you doing here?'

'What I've been doing this whole time – keeping you company.'

'But . . . But you can't be here. It was empty when they put me in. The door hasn't opened. This . . . This doesn't make sense . . .'

'Come on, Donald,' he said. 'It isn't hard to figure out. You're a very stable genius, right?'

I had an inkling, but I kept quiet.

Orange sighed. 'Oh, you're going to make me say it? Fine – I'm a figment of your imagination.'

A chill ran down my spine, which is very long and very straight.

'No,' I moaned, 'that's not true. That's impossible!'

'You're under huge mental strain, so you conjured up a friend. Why do you think I look and sound exactly like Morgan Freeman in that one movie? Because your boomer brain is addled with pop culture.'

'Wrong!' I said, starting to panic. 'Fake news!'

'Didn't you find it suspicious that a working-class African-American felon agrees with every one of your beliefs?'

'No. Blacks love Trump!'

Orange shook his head sadly. When he spoke, there was pity in his voice. 'I'm afraid that's not true. I do. But then, I'm you.'

'Wait, does this mean other people in my life are imaginary? Don Jr? Tell me Don Jr's a figment.'

'Sorry, he's real.'

'Goddammit!'

I was shaking now, sweat pouring down my face. I started to bargain.

'Okay, fine, so you don't exist or whatever. I can work with that. Let's make a deal – you keep being my friend and we never speak of this again.'

'Sorry, I can't accept that deal. Goodbye, Donald.'

He melted into the shadows, and once again I was alone. More alone than ever. The most alone anyone has been in our nation's history. Nobody is lonelier than Trump, believe me.

PART THREE

THE SMALLHAND
REDEMPTION

I really want to be a nice person. I am a nice person.

> – Donald Trump,
> speech in Nashville,
> Tennessee, 2015

17

Long Walk to Free Don

DAY TWO HUNDRED AND FORTY-FOUR

I had reached my lowest point. Lower than my bankruptcies in the early nineties. Lower than the *Access Hollywood* tape. And lower than when I lost the 2020 election. There, I said it – it wasn't stolen, I lost.

Sitting in that bare stone chamber, I found myself questioning every decision I've ever made. I had lived a big life – many say the biggest. And yet, looking back, it seemed so small. I may have earned billions, bedded top models and enjoyed the finest fast food the world has to offer, but none of it brought me happiness. No matter how much I acquired, it was never enough. Inside, I was as empty as this cell.

I had won fame and fortune, built monuments to myself, become the center of everyone's attention. So what? At the end of the day, it was all an act. Instead of being a person, I was playing the role of Trump. Maybe that's why I frequently referred to myself in the third person. Trump was a mask, a meme, a big con job.

I couldn't shake the thought that I had wasted my life. This terrified me at first. But as I came to accept it, I felt a huge sense of relief. The jig was finally up. I didn't have to be Donald Trump anymore. I didn't have to brag every time I opened my mouth, or live my whole life in superlatives. I could just be a guy. I could be me, whatever 'me' is.

And just because I was a world-historical shithead, I didn't have to keep being one. Even now, in middle age – by which I mean my late seventies – I could change. Make amends to those I'd hurt. Devote myself to good works. Perhaps even make this country a better place.

In my new, zen-like state, the days flew by. Before I knew it, Clint opened the door and I was led out, blinking and staggering. The captain of the guards gave me a guilty smile.

'Hope you're okay, Mr Trump. I gotta say, I'm not crazy about what we did to you.'

To his very great surprise, I embraced him. 'I forgive you.'

When I pulled away, he looked confused.

'Are you sure? I mean, I kind of stabbed you in the back. And, y'know, killed your friend . . .'

'Hey, as Jesus said, you've got to turn the other cheek. Which sounds like a spanking thing. Not that I'm into that. Stormy Daniels told *60 Minutes* she spanked me with a magazine that had my face on it. Fake news.'

And so I returned to my cell and updated my diary. Then I grabbed another strip of toilet paper and started planning good deeds. Believe me, these deeds are going to be so good. Possibly the best deeds of all time. And I'm going to be humble. Such tremendous humility. No one is more humble than Trump.

DAY TWO HUNDRED AND FORTY-FIVE

Today I visited the prison library for the first time. I've never been what you'd call a reader, unless it's the spicier bits of *Playboy* or an article about me. But I figured I have plenty of time on my hands. Why not try something new?

Anyway, the library isn't much to look at – just a back room with a bolted-down chair and a couple dozen books on rickety shelves. Alongside the Stephen Kings, Dan Browns and John Grishams, there were old copies of *Reader's Digest* and *National Geographic*. And tucked away on the bottom shelf, a familiar black cover stamped with gold foil. *The Art of the Deal*. I picked it up. The photo showed an expensively dressed forty-one-year-old man in front of Central Park, a smirk on his face. It was the Donald Trump of 1987. Before *The Apprentice*. Before the presidency. Before Smallhand. I thought, if only I could go back and tell him what I know now. Imagine all the suffering that could have been avoided, for myself and others. But maybe not. Maybe this had to happen for me to see the error of my ways.

With that in mind, I sat down and read *The Art of the Deal*. Turns out it's not half bad!

DAY TWO HUNDRED AND FORTY-SIX

In the spirit of trying new things, I've decided to start listening to people.* Doing this, I learned something incredible – there are interesting humans not called Donald J. Trump! And quite a few of them can be found right here at Smallhand. Just today, I spoke to an army veteran, a former football star and a chess grandmaster. Also, a man who claims he invented Minions, those little yellow guys with the goggles. Then he told me he was the first guy to walk on the moon – incredible.

---

* Historically, I just watch the other person's mouth move until it's my turn to talk again.

It's like everybody has their own story, a unique series of events that brought them to where they are. And if you ask about it, nine times out of ten they'll tell you. Of course, it's a struggle not to interrupt – the habits of a lifetime don't change overnight. But I find I can go about two minutes before jumping in. With practice, I'm hoping to get this up to three, four, maybe even five.

DAY TWO HUNDRED AND FORTY-EIGHT

In the yard, I got talking with a great guy, Brother Omar. He's African-American – the non-imaginary kind. I complimented him on his little white hat, which he said is called a kufi. I asked him where he got it. He said it was a religious thing. Islam. Then he asked if I would be up for receiving the light of Allah in my heart. I said absolutely.

He started taking me through the Five Pillars. The old me would have complained that there weren't enough pillars, that I need ten minimum. The new me kept his mouth shut and listened. Long story short, I'm a Muslim now. This makes me feel extra bad for banning us from the country. But, as it says in Surah An-Nur, the 24th chapter of the Holy Quran, 'Allah is All-Forgiving, Most Merciful'.

DAY TWO HUNDRED AND FIFTY

Once again, spent all my free time in the library.
Reading is doing wonders for my vocabulary.
I used to rely on a lexicon of roughly a hundred
words, chief among which were 'big', 'huge',
'bad', 'stupid', 'loser', 'fantastic', 'tremendous',
'incredible', 'classy', 'beautiful' and 'dumb'.
Occasionally I would get stuck and make up
terms, like bigly or covfefe. But now I express
myself in a far more elegant fashion. My idiolect
has become coruscating, erudite and ludic,
avoiding both the Scylla of obscurantism and
the Charybdis of ostentatious prolixity. It really
is tremendous. Very classy.

DAY TWO HUNDRED AND SIXTY-ONE

These conversations with my fellow prisoners
are having a profound effect on my political
views. I used to think that anyone who went

to jail was an animal, a worthless bastard who deliberately made bad decisions. This simply isn't the case. More and more I realize how constrained we are by external circumstances. Would I have got as far as I did if I'd been born to a single mother in a housing project, rather than a multi-millionaire real-estate developer? Probably, but it would have been tough.

Talking to marginalized people, I see the harm I've caused with my cruel words and damaging policies. And I regret – boy, do I regret. But regret won't help anybody. So I'm going to channel that feeling into something productive. I intend to become an advocate for prison reform and social justice more broadly. I've been reading Ta-Nehisi Coates and Robin DiAngelo, educating myself on bodies and spaces, intersectionality, all that jazz. Many are saying Trump is woke, arguably the wokest guy there's ever been.

I've learned a lot, and my supporters need to hear about it. Should I get the chance, I'll tell them that yes, we need to Make America Great. But what's keeping our country from greatness isn't Mexicans, political correctness or Antifa. It's the carceral state. It's structural racism. It's systemic inequality. If I put it like that, I'm sure the people who voted for me will change their minds.

DAY TWO HUNDRED AND NINETY-FOUR

Dear Diary, I haven't added to you much lately.
Sorry about that. I've been busy, you see –
helping other prisoners learn to read, studying
moral philosophy, praying toward Mecca. And
to be honest, I'm less interested in talking
about myself these days. But a couple of things
happened that I want to record. They put me in
mind of when I first came to Smallhand, so, so
long ago.

I was in the yard when the gates screeched
open. I looked across to see the gray prison
bus pull up. Out came a group of sorry-looking
fellas, chained together single-file. Inmates ran
to the chain-link fence, rattling it and howling
at the new arrivals.

'Fresh fish! Fresh fish! Hey, fishy, fishy, fishy!
We're gonna have a lot of fun with you, little
fishies!'

I watched the new guys get prodded along by
guards. They were dazed, trying to make sense
of their ruined lives. I felt compassion for these
lost souls. Compassion and sadness. A lifetime
ago, I was one of them.

Then I spotted a familiar figure in a silver
suit, heliotrope shirt and black-and-white
striped tie. It was McGill, my former lawyer. He
looked pale and haggard – clearly Mexico hadn't
worked out. Later, I ran into him in the mess

hall. He'd been outfitted with a bright orange jumpsuit, which was less loud than his usual get-up. On seeing me, he flashed his veneers.

'Mr President! How's things?'

'I'm tremendous, actually. And you?'

His bright smile faded.

'I've been better. Look, I just want to apologize. I said I'd get your conviction overturned. I'm sorry I let you down.'

I clapped a hand on his shoulder.

'Hey, these things happen. I'm sure you did as much as you could.'

'So you're not angry at me?'

I told him no. And I meant it. There was a time I would have been furious. But now I realize that everything turned out for the best. In Smallhand, I found an inner peace I never knew on the outside. Fundamental to this is acceptance – I accept that I belong in here.

18

A Bolt from the Red, White and Blue

DAY THREE HUNDRED AND FIVE

Part One

At breakfast, a couple of guards came up and
told me I had a visitor. But instead of taking
me to the usual visiting area – the one with all
the Plexiglas – they led me to a private room.
No barriers. Just a table, at which sat a bookish
young man in a spotty bow tie. He stood and
shook my hand.

'Mr President,' he said. 'My name is Tardis
Buckley. I'm a representative of the Republican
National Committee. May I say what an honor
it is to meet my political hero?'

'Thanks for coming out. Though, as you
might have heard, I retired from politics.'

I gestured at my orange jumpsuit.

'Your wrongful imprisonment is a national
disgrace, Mr President.'

'Listen, pal, you don't have to use titles. The
old me was president. Now I'm just Donald.'

The guy shot me an odd little smile. 'With all due respect, sir, you *are* president. Today is November sixth, 2024. The election was held yesterday. You won.'

. . .

I just sat there with my mouth hanging open for about ten minutes. Buckley was about to call an ambulance when I finally snapped out of it.

'How did this happen? Last I heard, I was on two percent in the primaries.'

'It's true that you struggled in the polls after getting locked up. But, like every Trump scandal, it blew over. Thanks to the . . . passion of your supporters, you won the nomination *in absentia*. It didn't hurt that your main rival was Ron DeSantis.'

Ah yes, Ron DeSanctimonious. Weird guy. Looks like a meatball, thinks Mickey Mouse is turning kids trans. No wonder I beat him without even trying.

'But what about the campaign?'

'Well, it seemed like a cakewalk for Biden. He just had to keep a low profile and remind voters that his opponent was literally a criminal. Then he made a huge mistake. The Democrats wanted to go ahead with televised debates, putting the president up against an empty podium. But without you there to interrupt him, Biden rambled for a full ninety minutes about his dad's Chevrolet Corvette and the price of a milkshake in 1958. It was a spectacular display of senility, and the public were greatly alarmed. This depressed turnout, allowing you to secure a win in the electoral college.'

All I could do was shake my head. 'I don't understand how any of this happened without me knowing.'

Buckley fingered his bow tie, looking a little awkward.

'The upper echelons of the Republican Party decided it would be best for the campaign if you weren't directly involved. No offense, Mr President. Also, Warden Snook was determined to keep you and your fellow prisoners in the dark. He felt knowledge of the wider political situation might cause instability at Smallhand.'

'Unbelievable. So what happens next?'

The kid took some official-looking papers out of his briefcase and slid them over to me.

'As President-elect, you are entitled to pardon yourself of all crimes, effective immediately. It's in the constitution – one of the boring bits that no one reads.'

He produced a very classy fountain pen and held it out.

'So what do you say, Mr President? Will you come back and lead America to glory?'

I stared at the pen, its clip glittering in the light. The events of the previous ten months ran through my head. The triumphs. The tragedies. The bowls of glop. And above all, the new life I had built for myself. A life of modesty and spiritual fulfillment. What would I be giving up if I returned to my former existence, with its glamor, razzmatazz and emptiness? Wasn't I so much happier now?

Then I thought, screw that shit.

Part Two

As soon as I completed my signature – which is very stylish and not a deranged squiggle like some people say – a strange feeling washed over me. It was like I had been asleep for hundreds of years and now, suddenly, I was awake. Awake, but not woke. In an instant, all that SJW crap fell away. Donald Trump was back, baby.

Tardis had brought some secret-service guys with him to defend the president-elect. I ordered them to escort me to the warden's office. Inside, Snook was kneeling beneath the crucifix on his wall, hands clasped in prayer. Clint stood nearby, pale and unshaven.

'Warden Snook?' I said. 'You're fired!'

He got to his feet, greeting me with his usual sneer. 'I've been expecting you, Prisoner #42069.'

'That's *Mr President*. And I bet you weren't expecting me to win the election.'

'God works in mysterious ways.'

'Well, he's not a fan of you, because you're screwed. You sent me to the Hole. Now I'm going to send you to a hole – a little place called Guantanamo Bay. And unlike most of the guys there, you actually did something.'

A couple of my secret-service thugs grabbed Snook and bundled him out of the room. Then I jabbed a long, presidential finger at the captain of the guards.

'Him too. Straight to Guantanamo.'

Clint fell to his knees. 'Please, Mr Trump – Snook made me do those things. And I felt just terrible. I mean, I'm your biggest fan . . .'

'Wrong! My biggest fan would never have done what you did. You tortured me. Killed my favorite goon. And worst of all, you burned a very expensive, very luxurious hairpiece. Take him.'

I was walking out of the warden's office when I heard a warm, silky voice.

'Sir? I just wanted to offer my congratulations.'

I turned to see Orange smiling at me, a cloth cap in his hands, like the one Morgan Freeman wears in that movie – *The Stickshift Reduction? The Shithouse Reunion?* Honestly, I couldn't concentrate. Not enough fight scenes and no babes to speak of. Total sausage party.

'What the heck?' I said. 'I thought you were a figment.'

'That may well be the case. Still, I consider you a friend, and I'm happy for you.'

'Thanks. And thanks for everything. You may have been imaginary, but your love was real.'

Orange smiled, a little bashful. 'I guess this is goodbye.'

'I guess so.'

'Goodbye, sir.'

I turned to walk away. Then I turned back. 'We worked well together, didn't we? Running the Deplorables?'

'We did indeed.'

'Y'know, it's gonna be tough re-draining the swamp and Making America Great Again again. I could use a little help. How about I give you that pardon?'

His wise eyes filled with dignified tears. 'That's awful kind, but you don't need to. I'm just someone you dreamed up. If you think about me in the White House, I'll appear.'

'Great,' I said. 'Maybe I'll give you a cabinet position. That would be historic – the first imaginary Secretary of State.'

Buckley informed me that a helicopter had been called to whisk me to Mar-a-Lago. This was welcome news. But I needed to see one more person before I split.

'Hi, Doc,' I said, sweeping into Conti's office.

'Mr Trump,' she said. Her face had a gray undertone and she looked about ten years older. This would put her in her late fifties, which – I'm sorry – is not an acceptable age for a woman.

'I know we don't have an appointment, but I thought, under the circumstances, you could squeeze me in.'

'Take a seat,' she said through gritted teeth.

For the last time, I sat down in one of her cheap, very not-plush chairs.

'So I'm guessing you didn't vote for me yesterday?'

'Correct.'

'That's okay. I still won by a historic landslide. Huge.'

'You must be delighted.'

'Sure I am. But I was wondering something. When you cut off our sessions, was that because I got the nomination?'

She nodded, not a happy camper. 'If there was a chance of you becoming president again, I didn't want to be complicit.'

'Yeah, well, that was dumb. If you'd just been nice to me, you could have appealed to my better angels. Maybe I would've made you official therapist to the president. But now you've hurt my feelings, who knows what I'll do? Ban psychiatry? That would make the Scientologists very happy.'

The shrink stared at me for a long time. When she spoke, her voice had a steely quality. 'I appreciate your coming to see me, Donald. As your therapist, I'd be happy to offer one last assessment.'

I snorted. 'Knock yourself out.'

'You are . . . a truly remarkable human being.'

'Tell me something I don't know.'

'Unfortunately, none of those remarks are positive. Time and again, you bend the world to your will – this election is only the latest example. However, your victories come at a terrible price. You can drag people down, but you can't lift yourself up. You can make your society more fractured, contentious and miserable, but you can't improve it. You're fond of applying superlatives to yourself – strongest, smartest, richest. Allow me to apply one. Donald, you are the emptiest man alive.'

I didn't dignify that bullshit by engaging with it. I just got up and delivered a brutal parting shot.

'Bye-bye, honey! You're very nasty!'

And so I walked back to my cell for the last time. A bottle of fake tan and a new hairpiece had been laid out on my cot. Buckley brought in a mirror and I set about restoring my look. Soon I was back to myself – Donald J. Trump, 45th and 47th President of the United States, the ultimate winner. It was like my stay in Smallhand had never happened.

As I write this, I can hear a helicopter landing in the yard outside. It will take me straight to Mar-a-Lago, where I will immediately begin planning for the presidential transition. Well, first I'll get a Happy Meal, play a round of golf and watch eight or so hours of Fox News. But then it's down to work.

Word of my victory must have spread, because now all the prisoners in my cell block are chanting.

'Trump! Trump! Trump!'

'Four more years! Four more years!'

God knows why they're excited. Maybe they think life will get better with one of their own in the White House. If so, they're dumber than I thought. All that stuff I said about prison reform and ending the carceral state? Null and void. Why would I do anything for these deadbeat crooks? If they really wanted to get out, they'd do what I did and accidentally win a presidential election.

In fact, I plan to expand the prison population very strongly. I'm gonna lock up all my political rivals, along with anyone who has, at any point, mocked or opposed me. Lock 'em up and throw away the key. I intend to build thousands of ultra-hyper-maximum-security prisons, the likes of which we've never seen in this country. I'm picturing the magnetic jail from *Face/Off*. Or the pit where they put Batman in *The Dark Knight Rises*. That would be cool.

Okay, it's nearly time to leave. What have I learned from my experience? The answer – and this may surprise you – is nothing. Nothing at all. As ever, I was totally one hundred percent right from the beginning, and there's no reason for me to change or grow. Changing and growing is for losers.

Yep, I haven't learned a thing. How could I? I never even went to prison. That was fake news. Sad!

THE END

AND, FRANKLY, IT'S A GREAT END

MAYBE THE GREATEST WE'VE SEEN
IN THIS COUNTRY

WHICH IS BEING RECOGNIZED
MORE AND MORE

BY ALL THE TOP PEOPLE

VERY SMART GUYS, BELIEVE ME.

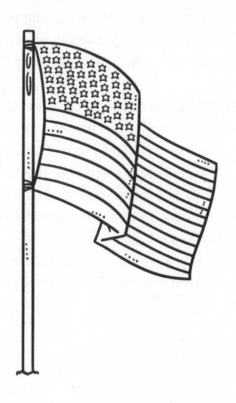